Welcome to Our French Table

A cookbook from the Central Baptist Church

Perpignan, France

Self-edited and translated by the
Evangelical Association of Perpignan
7 rue Pierre Talrich
66000 Perpignan, France

Welcome to Our French Table, by members of the Perpignan Central Baptist Church, has been translated and adapted for the American public from the original ***Bienvenue à Notre Table.***

All recipe measurements have been converted to fit standard American kitchen measuring utensils.

All pictures are our own photographs.
Cover photo: Collioure, a beautiful Catalan coastal village not far from our own Perpignan, renowned for inspiring many famous artists.

All Scripture references are taken from the Original King James Version of the Bible.

Many thanks to the test cooks from the Crossroads Baptist Church (Cincinnati, OH) and the Lakeside Baptist Church (Lakeville, IN) who have helped perfect the recipes for the American kitchen and thank you to those who have served as editors for our American text.

ISBN: 978-0-615-63078-6
June 2012

Ordering Information:

If you would like to order one or more copies of this cookbook, please contact us at the following email address:

cookbook@eglise-baptiste-perpignan.org

Or order directly from our church website

http://www.eglise-baptiste-perpignan.org

Click on the American flag for English

Eglise Baptiste du Centre *Perpignan*

Forward

Our initial reason for making a church cookbook was the desire to raise money to be able to one day, according to God's will, become owners of our own church building. God, in His wisdom, certainly saw other reasons not any less important, like gathering together regularly for the preparation of this book. It resulted in hours of exchanged fellowship, sharing, and laughter in order to reach our goal.

In this cookbook we present you with our best recipes. Our recipes are ones that we especially enjoy or that have stood the test of time. Because of the vast variety that comprises this cookbook, we are sure that you will find some recipes pleasing to your tastes.

You won't find any other culinary composition like ours in the world. Our collection of recipes is unique because our book represents our local church in Perpignan, France, which is comprised of people from diverse backgrounds, cultures, and culinary habits, united together in one fellowship through one faith in the Lord Jesus Christ.

This book took teamwork with everyone participating. Every cook presents their recipe with their own method of preparation. Each recipe was corrected by the contributing person. Despite our attentiveness to detail in corrections and translations, please excuse any slight errors that may have escaped our attention.

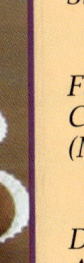

Chapters

Recipe Index   6

Special Ingredient Information   10

Cold First Courses: Appetizers and Small Plates   23

Hot First Courses: Soups, Appetizers, Small Plates, and Tarts   43

French Regional Cooking (Main Courses)   67

Dishes from Around the World (Main Courses)   91

French Desserts   117

Desserts from Around the World   153

French Missionary Ministries Information   178

Recipe Index

Cold First Courses

Avocado Melon Salad	24
Tomato Charlottes with Shrimp	26
Shrimp-Filled Grapefruit	28
Roasted Eggplant and Red Peppers—Catalan-style	30
Guacamole	32
Eggplant Spread	34
Tuna Olive Cake	36
Smoked Salmon Stuffed Cherry Tomatoes	37
Fresh Spring Rolls	38
Gazpacho	41

Hot First Courses

French Pistou Soup	44
Crème DuBarry (Cream of Cauliflower)	46
Carrot Velouté	48
Hungarian Onion Soup	49
Sautéed Sea Scallops and Leek Fondue	50
Honey Braised Leeks	52
Warm Goat Cheese Salad	54
Onion Tart	55
Five Grain Cereal Mix Pastry Shell	56
Express Pastry Crust	57
Tuna, Tomato, and Mozzarella Tart	58
Coca (Red Pepper Turnovers)	60
Carrot, Zucchini, and Cumin Puff Pastry Tart	62
Cheese Soufflé	64

French Regional Cooking

Catalan Chicken	70
Boles de Picoulat (Catalan Meatballs)	72
Ratatouille—Provence	74
Ratatouille and Tuna Tart	78
Gratin Dauphinois (Potatoes au Gratin)	79
Gratin Savoyard (Mashed Potatoes)	80
Stuffed Cabbage—Auvergne	82
Quiche Lorraine	85
Munster Valley Pie—Vosges Mountains	86
Normandy Chicken	88

Dishes from Around the World

Pineapple Pork—Asian	92
Thailand-Style Rice	94
Sautéed Vegetables in Oyster Sauce—Asian	96
Pork Spring Rolls—Vietnamese	99
Colombo (Martinique-Style Curry Chicken)	102
Gourmet Salad—exotic	104
Seafood Enchiladas—Mexican/American	106
Tandoori Chicken—Indian	108
Moussaka—Greek	110
Couscous—North African	112
Cumin Meatballs—Middle East influenced	115

French Desserts

Cream Puffs	118
Chocolate Truffles	122
French Macarons—base recipe, chocolate, vanilla buttercream, and raspberry fillings	124
Walnut Tart	131
Floating Islands	132
Alsatian Christmas Spice Cake	134
Crêpes	136
Far Breton (Prune Custard Cake)	138
Lemon Tart	140
Chocolate Cake	142
Gluten-Free Chocolate Cake	144
Apricot Cake	146
Yogurt Cake	148
Confiture de Lait (Milk Jelly)	150
Eve's Cake	151

Desserts from Around the World

Sévillan Cake—Spain	154
Macrouds—Morocco	156
Gazelle Horns—Morocco	158
Nam Van—Laos	160
Carmel Pineapple Upside Down Cake—Martinique	162
Tiramisu—Italy	164
Carrot Cake—America	166
Christmas Cake—England	168
Feuerwehr-Kuchen—Germany	171
Zucchini Bars—America	174
Lemon Curd—English	175

We would like to dedicate this cookbook to our dear sister in Christ, Jeannine Picole. Her unfailing faith in Christ and her love for others in spite of physical suffering was an encouragement and a strong example for all of us.

The French people are passionate about food. While some very elaborate family dinners on special occasions can have up to six courses, a traditional French meal is composed of a first course (also known as an entrée), main course, salad, cheese, and dessert. Most entrées may also be served as a main dish if you wish.

Many French cooks make their cuisine "au pif," which means "roughly guessing." In other words, they use their intuition, instead of fussing with measurements. They throw in the herbs and seasonings, adjust the salt and pepper to taste, and somehow their cooking instincts produce a wonderful, delicious aroma that emanates from the kitchen. It is an art that is very hard to measure in spoons and cups! We have done our very best to diligently measure the ingredients in American standard measurements. We have carefully researched ingredient equivalents in the states to make the most authentic recipes.

We consider this book a guide to help you step by step in your culinary adventures. We do our best to give you the right baking times. However, we encourage you to use your own judgment on cooking times. Ovens and stovetops may vary greatly. So don't hesitate to bake a tart for 10 minutes more or less if needed.

Some cookbooks contain adages, amusing stories, or famous quotes. We have chosen to include verses from the Bible, the book that we cherish more highly than any other. However, this recipe book remains first and foremost a French-influenced cuisine delight.

Bon appétit! From our French table to yours.
Kimberly Sauvage
Translator for the Evangelical Association of Perpignan

Things to know before starting

Flour: We recommend using cake flour for some of our baking recipes where specified. Other recipes use all purpose flour where we have judged necessary. **We have adapted and tested all of the recipes containing both all purpose flour and cake flour to ensure the final outcome of the recipes.**

Butter: Unless otherwise indicated, all our recipes use unsalted butter. You could probably still use salted butter in many of them and reduce the salt quantity elsewhere in the recipe. However, for our dessert recipes, which usually contain higher quantities of butter, *we highly recommend using unsalted butter.*

Eggs: All eggs are large eggs.

Pinch of salt: Many recipes call for a pinch of salt or pepper or some other spice. This usually means 1/8 teaspoon. However the French tend to season their dishes with less salt. We encourage you to salt and season to taste while making the recipe.

Measurements: You can be flexible with vegetable quantities. We have given the approximate weight simply as a guideline. Slightly more or less will not alter the outcome of most recipes. However, try to be precise when measuring flour quantities for desserts.

Express pastry crust: Several of our tart recipes require an ***express pastry crust.*** It is quick to make requiring only a bowl with an airtight firm fitting lid and a rolling pin. It's great not only for savory tarts, but also for sweet tarts.

Parchment paper: We line the pie pans or quiche pans of our tarts with this nonstick cooking paper or a wax paper that can resist oven temperatures.

Oven: Unless otherwise indicated, our cooking instructions are for a conventional oven with top and bottom heat. If you have a convection oven where the air is circulated with a fan, you may need to slightly reduce the temperature and cooking time.

Special ingredients from your local supermarket that you will need for certain recipes in this book:

Most of the recipes in this book can be made with ingredients that anyone should be able to find at a large supermarket. Fortunately, large grocery stores now have foreign food aisles and imported products that will allow you to have the closest results to all of the authentic recipes in this book. We have listed for you the most unfamiliar ingredients and where to find them in order to save you time on your shopping trips.

Emmentaler cheese: This Swiss cheese commonly used in France melts easily which makes it nice to use in sauces. You can find it in the imported cheese section of your larger grocery stores. However you can substitute any other quality Swiss style cheese less expensive than the imported cheeses.

Used in our **Tuna Olive Cake; Cheese Soufflé; Tuna, Tomato, and Mozzarella Tart; Onion Tart; Ratatouille and Tuna Tart; and our Greek Moussaka**

 **Fine grade semolina flour, or Semolina pasta flour:** Its golden sandy texture actually more closely resembles cornmeal than an actual flour. Don't confuse this with polenta. Semolina is processed from durum wheat and is often used in Arabic and Indian desserts as well as in Italian pasta making. You should be able to find it in the baking aisle of a large supermarket or you can buy it online. It is relatively inexpensive. We have also found it in bulk food stores in some Amish regions.

Used in our Morrocan dessert **Macrouds**

Couscous grain: You should be able to find this North African staple next to the rice and pasta, but it might also be found in the international food aisle. Don't confuse it with Israeli couscous which has a larger texture.

Used in our **North African Couscous**

Double concentrated tomato paste: Double concentrated tomato paste has a deeper, fuller tomato flavor than the single concentrated paste. Because it comes in a tube and keeps for a very long time in the refrigerator,

it is definitely worth the money. However, if you only have single concentrated paste on hand, don't worry. Just double the amount given in the ingredient list. It will not significantly change the recipe.

Used in our **Catalan Meatballs and North African Couscous**

Puff pastry: You will find this in the frozen section of your supermarket. One box usually contains two pastry shells. _It is definitely worth buying a name brand._ Simply thaw according to package directions before baking. Once thawed, you may also gently roll it out on parchment paper to the desired diameter. Do not leave the thawed pastry in a warm area for an extended period of time or it will become difficult to work with.

Used in our **Carrot, Zucchini, and Cumin Puff Pastry Tart; Munster Valley Pie; and Walnut Tart.** Can also be used in our **Coca (Red Pepper Turnovers) and Quiche Lorraine**

Mascarpone: This Italian cheese can be found in the imported cheese section of your grocery store. Although it is rather expensive, the flavor is necessary for our Tiramisu.

Ladyfingers: These softer cookies are usually found in the bakery/deli or dairy section of the supermarket, although sometimes they can be found in the foreign food aisle or even the cookie aisle. It is usually easier just to ask for this one.

Used in our Italian dessert **Tiramisu**

Crème Fraîche (Thick fresh cream): This cream looks much like sour cream, but don't be fooled. Although in some recipes you might get away with substituting sour cream for the crème fraîche, sour cream will curdle if used in cooking sauces. You can now purchase crème fraîche near the imported cheese section in some larger supermarkets. Though this heavenly cream is worth the money, you can *easily make a close substitute yourself at home* for much less.

Mix 1 cup heavy whipping cream with 1 Tbsp buttermilk or plain yogurt, or 1 Tbsp from a previous batch of homemade fresh cream. Cover and set aside in a warm spot for 12-24 hours until thickened. Cover and refrigerate. This crème fraîche will last for up to one week in the refrigerator. Try to find whipping cream that is not ultra-pasteurized. Don't worry about letting it sit out. The bacteria naturally present make this a safe process.

Must be used in our **Hungarian Onion Soup, Sautéed Sea Scallops and Leek Fondue, Onion Tart, Normandy Chicken, Ratatouille and Tuna Tart, Chocoate Truffles, and Walnut Tart**

Almond meal or almond flour: A few of our desserts will call for a certain quantity of almond flour. Almond flour is actually almonds that have been ground to a fine powder. You should be able to find it in the baking aisle of a large supermarket. It is available online as well, but ***you can also easily make it at home in your food processor or a small blender.*** If you know you'll be doing some recipes with almond flour, make it ahead of time in large quantities and freeze it. It will keep a couple of months. As long as you don't compress it when you freeze it, it is easy to scoop out the desired amount. ***One 16 oz. bag of almonds will make about 4 1/2 cups of almond flour.***

You can use blanched or unblanched raw almonds unless white almond flour is in the ingredient list. Then you will need to use the blanched almonds.

Fill your food processor bowl with a blade attachment about 2/3 full. Use the pulse button to grind them until you get a cornmeal consistency. Don't overgrind though, or you will get almond butter. Put the ground almonds through a flour sifter into a bowl. Any pieces left can be put back into the blender to grind some more.

Used in our **Macarons, English Christmas Cake, German Fireman's Cake, Morrocan Macrouds, and Gazelle Horns**

Available in meat markets

Morrocan/Mergueza sausages and lamp rib chops (or blade chops): These meats often used in North African cuisine can only be found in a special meat market. Mergueza sausages are usually made with lamb or a combination of beef and lamb.

Used in our **North African Couscous**

Ingredients that you may need to purchase from a local specialty store or online:

There are a few ingredients that may need to be found at a local fresh market or co-op which carries European ingredients. Some ingredients might need to be ordered online, depending on your supplier. To make it easier for you, we have listed the ingredients with the recipes in the book that call for them. It might take more time and a little more money, but these recipes are worth it for those special occasions that will leave a lasting impression.

To save you time from searching online, each bold print title is also the key words needed for your search engine to find the right online source page.

Couscous spice mix: This special blend of oriental spices such as peppercorns, ras el hanout, ginger, and more, gives that authentic taste to our Couscous recipe. You can probably only find it online.

Used in our **North African Couscous**

Harissa condiment in tube: For those who enjoy extra heat, this spicy North African hot chili paste is an authentic finishing touch.

Optional in our **North African Couscous**

Tandoori seasoning: Tandoori is actually the term for slow cooking in a clay oven. If you don't have an Indian market near you, this spice blend is available at any online spice company.

Used in our **Tandoori Chicken**

Used in our **Martinique Colombo**

Colombo spice blend: This French West Indies curry powder is extremely hard to find. Only a handful of online spice companies carry it. Or you can find out how to make it by typing Colombo powder on your Internet search engine. Another option would be to order through a British spice company.

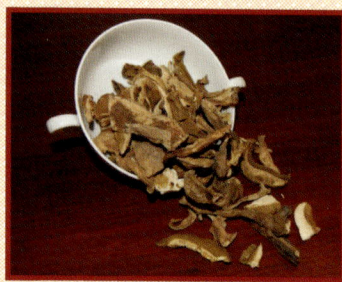
Used in our **Catalan Meatballs**

Dried porcini mushrooms (for cooking and baking): Also known as cèpes, this mushroom commonly used in Italian cooking gives a rich full flavor to one of our Catalan dishes. They are pretty pricey in gourmet stores. However, you can find them online without breaking your piggy bank.

Vanilla sugar packets (sucre vanillé): This common ingredient in French and European desserts is nothing more than sugar that has been infused with vanilla beans. You can easily buy packets of it online. *However, it remains optional. You may substitute 1 teaspoon vanilla extract for every packet called for in a recipe.*

Cardamom and Coriander powder: These rather unfamiliar spices to the Western hemisphere can easily be found in a fresh market, co-op, or at an online spice company for a reasonable price.

Used in our Morrocan dessert **Macrouds**

Five grain hot cereal mix: We used a multigrain hot cereal mix in a unique way in our five grain cereal mix pie shell. Although we used a five grain mix, any variety of whole rolled grains such as rye, barley, oats, and wheat will work. You can even use an organic mix. While you might be  able to find this in a health food store, it might be easier to order online. Several companies carry it. One bag will make several healthy pie shells for entrées, main courses, or even desserts.

Used in our **Five Grain Cereal Mix Pastry Shell**

 **Candied lemon peel:** This ingredient can be found in a gourmet store but is more easily found online. You can buy it diced as well which might be less expensive. The more ambitious cook can even make it. Directions are easily available online.

Used in our **Alsatian Christmas Spice Cake**

Orange flower water (or orange blossom water): Orange blossoms are distilled into a clear perfumed liquid to make orange flower water. This delicious flavoring is used in many French and Mediterranean desserts. It is available online. The purchase is well worth it for those authentic unique desserts that no one else can make.

Used in our two North African pastries, **Macrouds**, **Gazelle Horns**, and optional in our West Indies **Carmel Pineapple Upside Down Cake**

Ingredients that you may need to find in your local Asian market:

Some ingredients in our Asian recipes may be found in the foreign food aisle of your grocery store, but others must be purchased at an Asian market.

Black fungus (wood ear mushroom): This dehydrated Chinese mushroom is sold in a plastic bag and can be kept indefinitely. Once soaked in water, it puffs up 4-5 times its size.

Used in our **Pork Spring Rolls** and **Sautéed Vegetables in Oyster Sauce**

Rice and bean thread vermicelli: These inexpensive noodles look very similar. One is made from rice and the other from soybeans. It should be clearly marked on the package.

Used in our **Spring Rolls** as a first course and in our **Pork Spring Rolls**

Green pearl tapioca: This can only be purchased in an Asian market. However, you could substitute the regular small white pearl tapioca found in any large supermarket.

Used in our **Nam Van Tapioca Dessert**

Chinese pork sausage : These sweet, fatty, cured sausages are known as "lap chong" or as "kun chiang" in Thailand. They are widely used in Thai cuisine. They are not cooked yet, so you definitely need to cook them before eating.

Used in our **Thailand-Style Rice**

Recipe listing of special ingredients:

Here is a list of all twelve recipes in this book that have **special ingredients not always available in large supermarkets**. Most of these items have been explained on the previous pages. Buying certain spices as a group might be an easier way to try some of these recipes without spending a considerable amount of money.

Recipes	Special Ingredients
Spring Rolls as a first course	Pork meatloaf
Catalan Meatballs	Dried porcini mushrooms
Tandoori Chicken	Tandoori spice powder
Couscous	Lambchops, Mergueza sausages, couscous spice powder, and harissa (optional)
Pork Spring Rolls	Black fungus
Thai Rice	Chinese pork sausage
Sautéed Vegetables in Oyster Sauce	Black fungus
Colombo	Colombo spice powder
Alsatian Christmas Spice Cake	Candied lemon pieces
Macrouds	Cardamom and coriander spices, orange flower water
Gazelle Horns	Orange flower water
Nam Van	Green pearl tapioca

Kitchen utensils you will need to make several of our recipes

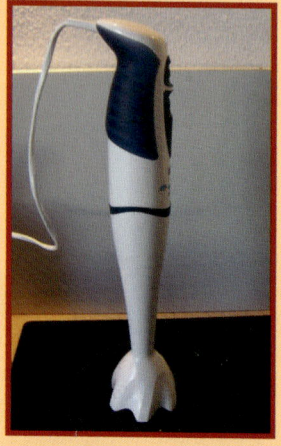

Immersion blender (hand blender): This *must have* utensil found in every French kitchen plunges directly into the food to blend or puree. It saves time and hassle by mixing hot foods directly in the saucepan rather than transferring them to a blender. You'll definitely want to use this for several of our soup recipes and you'll come to love it to blend hot or cold sauces in any other recipe.

Used in our **Pistou Soup, Cream of Cauliflower, Carrot Velouté, Hungarian Onion Soup, and Gazpacho.**

Food mill: While all of our soups are made with an immersion blender, this efficient kitchen device gives our soups an even smoother consistency. It is optional, but we recommend it. A simple one that sits easily on top of a pan or a bowl will be fine.

Can be used in our **Cream of Cauliflower, Hungarian Onion Soup, and Gazpacho.**

Quiche dish and a large round cake pan: If you're planning on baking cakes, quiches, or tarts in this book, you will want to invest in a 10 x 2 inch round cake pan and a 10 inch round ceramic quiche dish.

You will need a small soufflé dish for our Cheese Soufflé, and a 10 inch spring form pan for our German Fireman's Cake. All other pans or utensils are what most cooks already have in their kitchen.

Quantity: *We give you the approximate number of people you can serve with the quantities given in the ingredient list. However, we do not suggest a preparation time, which is usually unrealistic, depending on each person's schedule.*

Chef's Hat: *This small box gives good tips and advice from our cooks on how to successfully make the recipe.*

Our Photos: *Our numbered pictures show you the way your food preparation should look step by step as you make the recipe.*

The Best from the Rest: *The French word for leftovers is "les restes," the "rest of the food." Sometimes we give you an idea how to use the left over food in a recipe.*

Cold First Courses

Avocado Melon Salad

Monique Ospel

This extraordinary salad owes its distinctiveness to a delicious mango chutney vinaigrette.

Serves 4

Ingredients for the salad:
1 heart of lettuce
14-15 oz. cooked shrimp
1-2 ripe avocados
1 Tbsp lemon juice
2 1/2 cups cubed honeydew melon

Ingredients for the vinaigrette:
1 very heaping Tbsp spicy mango chutney (*foreign food aisle*)
2 Tbsp cider vinegar
2 Tbsp fresh squeezed orange juice
4 Tbsp olive oil
1/4 tsp salt
1/8 tsp pepper
1 1/2 Tbsp sesame seeds

1. Wash the lettuce leaves and peel the shrimp.

2. Open the avocado, take out the seed, and cut the avocado into cubes. Pour the lemon juice over the avocado cubes.

3. Cut open the melon, scrape out the seeds, and remove the rind. Cut the melon into large cubes.

4. Layer the lettuce leaves on the bottom of small plates or bowls. Top with the melon and avocado cubes.

5. In a small bowl, mix the mango chutney with the vinegar and the orange juice. Add the olive oil, salt, and pepper. Stir together with a whisk to blend it well. Pour the sesame seeds into the vinaigrette and stir again.

6. Spoon the vinaigrette over the salads.

7. Finish by nicely arranging the shrimp on top of the salads.

You may add other kinds of melon to the salad to vary the colors.

You could also replace the shrimp with cubed chicken or shredded crabmeat.

Mango chutney, which looks a lot like a jam, often accompanies Indian dishes. You should find it in the foreign food aisle of your larger supermarket.

Tomato Charlottes with Shrimp

Cathy Scotto

This appetizer is easy and refreshing in spite of it's refined appearance.

Serves 4

Ingredients:

24 medium cooked shrimp, (or cooked prawns)
8 Batavia lettuce leaves
2 1/2 Tbsp walnut or hazelnut oil (*must be refrigerated*)
2 lbs. medium size tomatoes, like Romas
1 Tbsp cider vinegar
2 Tbsp olive oil
salt and pepper
1 sprig fresh parsley
3 fresh chive stems
several fresh basil leaves

Reserve 4 shrimp for decoration if you wish and shell the others.

1 Wash the lettuce leaves, then thinly slice them into a bowl.

Mix the walnut or hazelnut oil with the lettuce leaves. Salt to taste, then set aside.

2 Cut some of the tomatoes into thin slices, enough to line the bottom of 4 small bowls or ramekins (5 inches in diameter) which serve as a mold for the charlottes.

3 Layer the reserved lettuce leaves over the tomato slices lining the bowls. Fill up these bowls about halfway with lettuce. Place 5 peeled shrimp on top of the lettuce in each bowl.

Peel and seed the remaining tomatoes cutting them into small cubes in a mixing bowl.

4 In a separate small mixing bowl, mix together the vinegar, olive oil, and a pinch of salt and pepper. Add the parsley leaves, the chive stems, and the basil leaves, all finely chopped.

5 Pour this vinaigrette over the tomato cubes and stir together.

6 Cover the shrimp in the bowls with this tomato mixture, pressing down a little with a spoon.

Cover the bowls with aluminum foil, then stack them on top of each other. Press down firmly on the stack of bowls, then put a fifth bowl on the top bowl weighted down with something. Put the stack of bowls in the refrigerator for at least 30 minutes.

Before serving, turn the bowls over onto a plate and gently unmold the tomato charlottes. Decorate with a whole shrimp if desired.

> *You can prepare the tomato charlottes the night before. Simply do not turn over the bowls onto a plate until just before serving.*

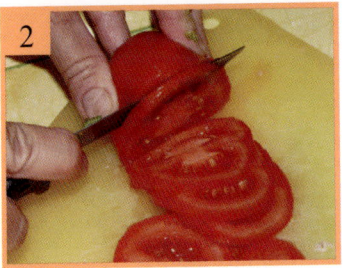

Shrimp-Filled Grapefruit

Jean Marc Sauvage

These stylish grapefruit are refreshing and surprisingly simple.

Serves 6

Ingredients:

3 pink or yellow grapefruit
12-14 oz. small cooked shrimp, drained
1 cup mayonnaise
3/4 cup ketchup
small fresh parsley sprigs for decoration (*optional*)

1. Cut the grapefruit into halves.

2. Squeeze the juice from the grapefruit, preferably with a juicer or the citrus press on your food processor. You can keep this juice for something else, but be sure to keep the pulp that is left in the sieve to use later in the recipe.

3. With a grapefruit spoon, take out all of the pulp left on the inside of the grapefruit down to the white rind. Keep this pulp as well. Reserve the empty grapefruit shells for serving.

4. Take the pulp that was left in the sieve of the citrus press along with the pulp from the inside of the grapefruit and purée them in your food processor or with an immersion blender.

5. Add the thawed and drained shrimp to the puréed pulp. Mix together.

Make the sauce by mixing together the mayonnaise and the ketchup.

6. Add this sauce to the grapefruit and the shrimp and stir together. Taste and add 1-2 Tbsp sugar if the mixture seems too bitter, which depends on the sweetness of the grapefruit and personal taste.

7 Fill the grapefruit shells with this mixture. Decorate the top with small parsley sprigs. Keep in the refrigerator until serving.

A grapefruit spoon, also called an orange spoon, has sharp teeth on the end to help break the fruit's flesh from the rind.

If you don't like the bitterness of grapefruit, this recipe is also good with oranges. Just adjust the quantities slightly according to the size of the oranges.

Roasted Eggplant and Red Peppers Catalan-style

Laura Canfran

This authentic recipe is enjoyed as an appetizer, but it can also nicely accompany a barbecue.

Serves 8-10

Ingredients:

6 red bell peppers
 (6 oz. each)
3 small eggplants
 (8-9 oz. each)
6 garlic cloves
5 Tbsp olive oil
salt and pepper to taste

Roasting the Vegetables: Preheat your oven to 410° F. Wash the vegetables and cut the stems from the red peppers and eggplants. Put them in an oven-safe dish to cook for about 1 hour. *You will need to keep an eye on the oven. The cooking time is approximate and can vary from 55 minutes to 1 hour and 20 minutes, depending on the type of oven. If the vegetables start to burn, turn down the temperature a little.*

After taking the vegetables out of the oven, immediately cover the dish with aluminum foil for 15 minutes.

1 **Preparation:** Once cooled, peel the skin off the peppers over a soup plate or a shallow bowl. Discard the seeds.

2 Cut the peppers into thin strips with a pair of scissors and place them in a shallow dish.

3 Strain the pepper juice that remains on the soup plate and pour over the peppers to add moisture.

4 Peel the eggplants. Remove the seeds if you wish. Cut them into thin strips like the peppers and add them to the peppers in the dish.

5 Mince the garlic and gently mix it in with the peppers and eggplants.

6 Drizzle the olive oil over the vegetables and mix together very gently with a fork. Add salt and pepper to taste. Let the vegetables marinate in the refrigerator overnight if you can. They will taste even better. They will keep in the refrigerator for 3-4 days.

> *This recipe is even tastier if you can roast the vegetables on the grill.*

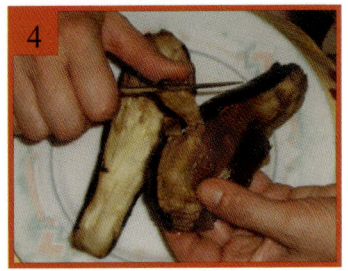

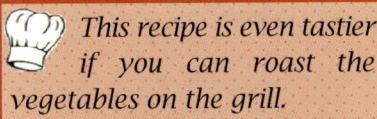

"The grass withereth, the flower fadeth: but the word of our God shall stand for ever."

Isaiah 40:8

Guacamole

Kimberly Sauvage

You'll never want to buy another jar of guacamole after tasting this Mexican avocado dip. It's packed with fresh flavors and is delicious on bread as well as tortilla chips.

Makes about 3 cups

Ingredients:

3 soft ripe avocados
1 1/2 Tbsp lemon juice
1 small shallot or onion
　　　(1/4 cup chopped)
2 large garlic cloves
sprigs of fresh cilantro
12 cherry tomatoes or
　　　1 small tomato
3/4 cup crème fraîche
　　　(or sour cream)
salt and pepper

1 Cut the avocados in half lengthwise around the pit. Scoop out the pit with the help of a spoon. Then scoop the avocado flesh out of the skins.

2 Mash the avocados until smooth with a fork or with an electric mixer. Stir in the lemon juice.

3 Prepare the remaining ingredients: dice the shallot, press the garlic, cut the fresh cilantro (a good handful) with scissors, and cut the cherry tomatoes into quarters or dice the tomato into small cubes.

4 Add the chopped shallot, garlic, and cilantro to the mashed avocado. Salt and pepper to taste.

5 Stir in the thick cream and then gently stir in the chopped tomato.

🧑‍🍳 *You can freeze the avocado purée before adding the other ingredients. The avocado keeps it's green color very well, which makes it possible to buy avocados in season and keep the purée in the freezer for up to six months. To freeze, follow the first two steps in our guacamole recipe. Put the purée into airtight freezer containers right away and put them in the freezer. If you would like to freeze more than three avocados, you need to calculate 1/2 Tbsp lemon juice per avocado. To make guacamole or any other recipe using avocado purée, take out of the freezer the night before and put it in the refrigerator. Let it finish thawing on the counter while you prepare the rest of the ingredients in the recipe.*

The Best from the Rest

If you have leftover guacamole that evening or the next day, stir it up to revive it's green color and put one spoonful on a tortilla. Don't spread it all the way out to the edges. Lay one slice of deli turkey and a few lettuce leaves or fresh cilantro leaves on top. Roll up the tortilla and cut it in half for a light meal. You could also make several and cut into bite sizes as an original finger food for a dinner or a picnic.

Eggplant Spread

Jacqueline Franco

This healthy recipe is excellent and lower in fat than the more modern eggplant spread recipes. It's a summer appetizer that is always appreciated!

Makes about 2 cups

Ingredients:

2 eggplants (about 9 oz. each)
5 small onions (around 1 1/2 oz. each)
1 large garlic clove
5 full sprigs of parsley
1 tsp coarse salt
pepper
1 Tbsp sunflower oil
juice from 1 lemon

Remove the stems from the eggplants and cut them in half lengthwise. Peel the onions.

Steam the eggplants and the peeled onions about 25 minutes or cook them 8-10 minutes in a pressure cooker.

1 Remove from heat once the eggplant's skin peels off easily with a knife.

When slightly cooled, peel all of the eggplants with the help of a knife. The skin should come off rather easily.

2 Cut the eggplants and the onions into large chunks before putting them in the blender.

Peel the garlic clove, cut it in half, and take out the center sprout.

3 Chop the parsley and the garlic clove together with a hand chopper or a food processor.

4 Add the chopped parsley and garlic to the chunks of eggplant along with the coarse salt, pepper, oil, and lemon juice.

5 Blend everything into a purée until there are no more chunks of onion. Season to taste.

Serve the spread cold on toasted bread or small party breads.

> 🧑‍🍳 This recipe is served in different ways, either as an appetizer with bread, or on small toasts for a cold buffet. The spread can also replace a vegetable served as an accompaniment to a main dish.

"Jesus answered and said, It is written, Man shall not live by bread alone, but by every word that proceedeth out of the mouth of God."

Matthew 4:4

Tuna Olive Cake

Kimberly Sauvage

This easy loaf cake is a very good choice for picnics, or served with a green salad for a light lunch.

Ingredients for 8-10 servings:

3 eggs
1 cup all purpose flour
1 Tbsp baking powder
2/3 cup milk
1/2 cup olive oil
1 1/2 cups grated emmentaler or gruyère cheese
2 cans tuna (5 oz. each), drained
1 cup green pitted olives

Preheat the oven to 350°F.

1 Beat the eggs together with the flour and the baking powder. Add the milk and olive oil. Mix together.

2 Add the grated cheese, drained tuna, and pitted olives. Stir together.

3 Pour into one large or two small greased loaf pans. If you are using a non-stick pan, you do not need to grease them. Bake for about 45 minutes to 1 hour or until an inserted toothpick comes out clean. Let the cake cool down slightly before removing from the pans. Serve warm or cold.

You may substitute salmon for the tuna and black olives for the green olives if you prefer.

Smoked Salmon Stuffed Cherry Tomatoes

Kimberly Sauvage

This pretty appetizer is nice as a finger food or to serve to guests on a bed of lettuce.

For about 30 cherry tomatoes

Ingredients:

30 cherry tomatoes
1/3 cup finely chopped onion
1/3 cup finely chopped green bell pepper
3 oz. smoked salmon
salt and pepper to taste
3 oz. cream cheese, softened
1 Tbsp milk
fresh sprigs of parsley or dill

1 Cut a thin slice off the top of each tomato. Scoop out the pulp.

2 Chop the onion and the green pepper. Cut the smoked salmon into small pieces.

In a small container, mix together the onion, pepper, smoked salmon and a pinch of salt and pepper. Stuff each tomato with this mixture.

3 In a small mixing bowl, combine the cream cheese and the milk until smooth. With the help of a pastry bag and a decorating tip, squeeze a small flower of cream cheese on top of each tomato. Garnish with parsley or dill sprigs.

Fresh Spring Rolls

Esther Sephanh

This Vietnamese appetizer is very easy to prepare. Its light, fresh texture is a nice alternative to fried spring rolls: just the right beginning to a meal.

For 4 spring rolls

Ingredients:
3 oz. fine rice vermicelli
　　(oriental style noodles)
2 imitation crab sticks
4 slices pork meatloaf,
　　thawed in the refrigerator
4 large lettuce leaves
1 sprig fresh mint
handful of bean sprouts
2 large cooked shrimp
4 rice wrappers

Preparation: Boil 4 1/2 cups water and add the rice noodles. Boil for about 8 minutes. *The rice vermicelli is cooked when it becomes sticky.* Pour the noodles into a colander and rinse them right away under cold water until they become cold to the touch.

1 Leave them in the colander over a bowl or in the sink for at least 20 minutes. Turn the noodles over once in a while to help them drain really well. During this time, prepare the other ingredients.

2 Cut the crab sticks in half, then cut again lengthwise.

3 Cut the pork loaf into about 1/4 inch thick slices. Take off the paper around the slices and cut them into small sticks.

4 Wash the lettuce leaves, the mint leaves, and the bean sprouts. Cut the shrimp in half lengthwise. Divide the drained vermicelli noodles into four piles.

Assemble the spring rolls using the steps that follow.

> *You can dip these in a spring roll sauce or a sweet and sour sauce.*

> *Leftover roast chicken or cooked pork is a delicious substitute for the pork meat loaf!*

Preparation:

The Best from the Rest

The spring rolls were good, but what are you going to do with the rest of the pork loaf? Vietnamese sandwiches, the French way. At work or on a picnic, its fresh flavors are so good.

Cut **one French baguette** in half lengthwise. Spread some **nuoc mam** and some **sweet and sour sauce** on the bread. Slice the remaining pork loaf to the desired thickness and lay it on the bread along with some **mint leaves and/or cilantro leaves**. Add a small **carrot** and half a **cucumber** which have been cut into julienne strips.

You should find the pork meat loaf in the freezer section of an Asian food market. It is marked "gio-lua" and it should also be marked "ready to eat" on the package. Simply thaw overnight in the refrigerator.

Wet two big kitchen towels. Wring them out very well and spread one towel out onto a workspace.

5 Immerse the rice paper into a pan filled with hot water for a few seconds and lay it on the towel. Repeat the process for the other three rice wrappers.

6 Cover them for several seconds with the other wet towel. *Be careful not to leave the towel on the rice papers too long.*

7 Put one shrimp and two pieces of imitation crab flattened between your fingers on each rice paper, *a little right of center.* Lay a lettuce leaf *on the left side.*

8 Put the rice vermicelli and the bean sprouts on top of the lettuce leaf.

9 Lay the pork slices and some mint leaves on top according to taste.

10 Fold over the opposite sides of the rice paper and roll it up very tightly. Serve cold. Keep them wrapped tightly in plastic wrap. They taste better fresh, but they can be kept wrapped in the refrigerator for up to 2 days.

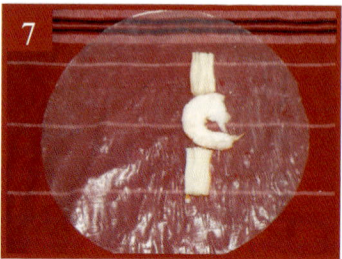

Gazpacho

Aurélie Scotto

This cold soup from the Andalucía region of Spain is not only enjoyed as a refreshing flavor packed appetizer on a hot summer day, but also as a healthy snack.

Ingredients for 6 servings:
portion of a stale French baguette (about 4 1/2 oz.)
3 cups cold water
2 1/2 lbs. tomatoes
10 oz. red bell peppers
4 large garlic cloves
1/4 cup olive oil
1 Tbsp vinegar
1 tsp salt
1 tsp pepper
basil leaves for decoration

1 Break the bread into large pieces in a deep bowl and add the cold water. Add the tomatoes cut into large chunks.

2 Seed the peppers, cut them into large chunks, and add them to the bowl. Peel the garlic and add the whole cloves to the bowl. Add the olive oil, vinegar, salt, and pepper.

3 Purée it all with an immersion blender. This will take a few minutes.

4 For an even smoother mixture, put it through a food mill. Decorate with several fresh basil leaves and serve cold.

Hot First Courses

French Pistou Soup

Cathy Scotto

This classic French garden soup would be just like any other ordinary vegetable bean soup if it weren't for its potent garlic and basil paste called pistou.

Serves 4

Ingredients for the soup:

8 1/2 cups water
1 carrot (3 1/2 oz.)
1 medium tomato (6 1/2 oz.)
2 small zucchini (13 1/2 oz.)
2 medium size potatoes (10 oz.)
1 lb. leeks (with green tops)
7 oz. fresh or frozen green beans
1 can (15 oz.) cannellini beans, partially drained
4 tsp salt, 1/4 tsp pepper
2 oz. spaghetti pasta

Ingredients for the sauce:

1 large ripe tomato
large handful of basil leaves
2 garlic cloves
1/2 cup parmesan cheese
1/4 cup olive oil

1 Cut all of the vegetables for the soup into small cubes.

2 In a pressure cooker, put the water, cubed vegetables, green beans broken into small pieces, salt, and pepper. Cook under pressure for 20 minutes.

3 Add the spaghetti pasta to the soup in small pieces (about 2 1/2 inches long) and boil uncovered for about 10 more minutes.

Add the partially drained cannellini beans, then turn off the heat.

The Sauce (Pistou):

4 In a bowl, put the tomato cut into large cubes, the basil leaves,

The Sauce:

whole cloves of garlic, and parmesan.

5. Mix it all together with an immersion blender. Add the oil and mix again.

Serve the hot soup accompanied by its basil sauce in a small side dish. Each person adds the desired amount of pistou to their bowl of soup.

The Coco Bean

The small white coco bean is traditionally used in the French Pistou Soup in France. The coco bean is practically impossible to find in the US, so we substituted a can of cannellini beans. In a pinch you could also substitute another canned white bean such as Great Northern or Navy beans.

You can use other kinds of pasta such as small macaroni or vermicelli. Simply cook the pasta according to the time indicated on the package.

Crème Dubarry
Cream of Cauliflower

Annette Dure

This French classic velouté, supposedly named after a Countess, is creamy and delicious.

Serves 4

Ingredients:

2 Tbsp unsalted butter
2 Tbsp all purpose flour
4 1/2 cups milk
1 1/2 tsp salt
pinch of pepper
grated nutmeg to taste
   (about 1/4 tsp)
1 cauliflower head
   (about 1lb. 5 oz.)
1/3 cup heavy whipping cream

Make a light white sauce with the butter, flour, and milk. (See opposite page). Season to taste with salt and pepper and grated nutmeg.

1. Cut off the florets of the cauliflower, wash and blanch them.

2. To blanch them, put them in a pot of cold water and bring the water to a boil. As soon as the water boils, drain the cauliflower in a colander.

3. Gently cook the florets in the white sauce for about 15-20 minutes. Stir from time to time.

When the cauliflower is cooked, purée it along with its white sauce with an immersion blender. Pass it through a strainer or a fine meshed food mill if you want an even smoother texture. Adjust the seasonings if needed. Mix in the whipping cream before serving.

How to Always Succeed with Your White Sauce

1. Melt the butter in a pan. Make the roux by mixing the flour and the butter with a wire whisk. Let it cook for 3 minutes while stirring.

3. Heat the milk in another pan. Slowly add the hot milk to the cooled roux while stirring with a wire whisk. Return the pan to the burner.

2. Cool down the roux in the pan immediately in the sink filled with cold water.

4. Mix until it comes to a boil. Boil for 2-3 minutes. Salt, pepper, and season with other spices such as grated nutmeg.

Carrot Velouté

Cathy Scotto

You can forget about those ready-made cans of soup with this delicious velouté.

Ingredients for 4 servings:

1 small onion (1/4 cup chopped)
6 carrots (about 1 lb.)
3 Tbsp olive oil
1 tsp salt, and 1/2 tsp pepper
1 bouillon cube, any kind (*optional*)
2 Tbsp heavy whipping cream
1 Tbsp all purpose flour
1 cup milk or water

Cut the onion into small pieces and the carrots into small sticks.

1 In the pressure cooker, brown the onion in 2 Tbsp olive oil. Add the carrots and let them cook while stirring for a couple of minutes. Add salt and pepper.

Add 3 cups of water along with the bouillon cube. Close the pressure cooker and pressure cook it for 45 minutes.

2 Open the cooker and purée with an immersion blender. Add the whipping cream.

3 In another pan, make a roux by mixing together the other Tbsp of olive oil and the flour. Add the soup little by little while stirring until all the soup has been added. If the mixture is too thick, add all or some of the 1 cup of milk or water, but be sure not to make the velouté too thin.

Hungarian Onion Soup

Jacqueline Franco

This hot soup is warming at the end of a very cold autumn or winter day.

Ingredients for 4 servings:

1 lb. 12 oz. onions (about 8 medium/large onions)
3 1/2 Tbsp butter
1/2 cup milk
1 chicken bouillon cube dissolved in 4 1/2 cups hot water
1 egg yolk
3 heaping Tbsp crème fraîche
2 Tbsp ground paprika

1. Peel and slice the onions. Melt the butter in a sauce pan, then add the onions along with the milk. Cook on low heat for about 25 minutes until the onions become translucent and can be easily crushed.

Purée them with an immersion blender. You can strain them through a food mill for a smoother texture if you wish.

2. Put all of the puréed onions back into a pan and mix them with the hot water and the dissolved bouillon cube.

3. Thin down the egg yolk in a small bowl with the fresh cream and the paprika.

Put this mixture into a warmed serving dish. Then pour in the hot onion soup and mix together. Serve the soup very hot sprinkled with paprika. Salt to taste.

Sautéed Sea Scallops and Leek Fondue

Jean Marc Sauvage

This appetizer is as easy as it is delicious, proving that refined can be simple.

Serves 8

Ingredients:

6 large whole leeks (about 4-5 lbs. with the green tops)
4 Tbsp and 1 1/2 Tbsp unsalted butter
salt and pepper (about 1 tsp each)
1 cup crème fraîche (fresh cream)
1 bag of fresh or frozen sea scallops *(3-4 per person)*

The leeks will shrink in size when cooked. Add salt and pepper to taste.

Take off most of the green from the leeks. Rinse them carefully to wash off the dirt in between the outside layers.

1. Cut them into about 1/2 inch thick slices.

2. Put 4 Tbsp butter into a pan. As soon as the butter melts, add the leeks. Stir gently, then cover and let them cook on reduced heat for about 15 minutes. Keep your eye on them and stir from time to time to prevent them from sticking to the bottom of the pan.

You can cook the leeks before the guests arrive and reheat them while you cook the sea scallops.

3. Mix the fresh cream in with the leeks. Let cook uncovered for another 5 minutes on reduced heat to allow water to evaporate.

4. Take the scallops out of the freezer about 1/2 hour before cooking them. Once thawed, melt the remaining 1 1/2 Tbsp butter in a pan. Add the scallops and cook for not more than one minute on each side on medium to high heat. The scallops will shrink greatly in size.

Serve hot on top of the leeks. If you have time, heat the plates a little in the oven for a perfect presentation.

The Best from the Rest

If you have leftover cooked leeks, the next day you can make a pizza with the leeks, topped with some smoked salmon. It's delicious! Or add the leftover leeks to our Quiche Lorraine (see page 85).

"*For the word of God is quick, and powerful, and sharper than any twoedged sword... and is a discerner of the thoughts and intents of the heart.*"

Hebrews 4:12

Honey Braised Leeks

Brigitte Kalms

These leeks, succulent for a small dinner, will also perfectly accompany a fish course during a special occasion.

Serves 4

Ingredients:

3 large leeks or 5-6 smaller leeks (about 1 lb. leeks when cut)
1/3 cup water
2 heaping Tbsp honey
6 Tbsp unsalted butter
3 pinches salt

Preheat the oven to 350° F.

1 Wash and cut the leeks diagonally into 2 inch long slices. If the leeks are large, cut the slices in half lengthwise. (You should have about 1 lb. cut leeks.)

2 Arrange the leeks tightly together in a pan suitable for both the stovetop and the oven. *Be careful to vary the colors. Insert the white leeks in between the green ones for a nicer presentation.*

Add the water little by little while the leeks cook on medium heat. Cook for about 7-8 minutes.

3 Slowly drizzle the honey uniformly over the leeks. Cook for another 7-8 minutes.

4 Add the butter cut into small pieces. Cook on slightly higher heat for another 7-8 minutes. The liquid will evaporate a little at a time.

5 Baste the leeks regularly with a spoon until about 3/4 of their liquid has evaporated. Add the pinches of salt at this time.

Transfer the pan to the oven and bake for 15-20 minutes.

6 Turn the leeks over and bake for another 15-20 minutes.

7 The leeks will turn a pretty caramel color during baking.

Serve very hot.

Jesus said..."Blessed are those who hear the word of God, and keep it!"

Luke 11:28

Warm Goat Cheese Salad

Kimberly Sauvage

This easy salad drizzled with a homemade vinaigrette and topped with warm goat cheese toasts is wonderful as a first course for guests or as a light dinner.

Serves 4

Ingredients for the vinaigrette:
2 tsp Dijon mustard
pinch of salt and pepper
2 Tbsp vinegar
6 Tbsp olive oil
1 Tbsp finely chopped shallot
1 Tbsp fresh chives or parsley

Ingredients for the salad:
salad greens, any kind
12 cherry tomatoes, cut in half
1 goat cheese log
3 bread slices
1 tsp thyme leaves
1 tsp honey

Preheat the oven to 425°F. Place the mustard in a small bowl. With a wire whisk, mix in a pinch of salt and pepper and the vinegar. Gradually add the olive oil while mixing. Stir in the shallot and chives.

1. Wash the salad greens and arrange them nicely on 4 plates along with the cherry tomatoes cut in half. Drizzle the vinaigrette over the salads.

2. Cut the bread slices into four triangles each and place them on a cookie sheet covered with parchment paper. Cut the goat cheese log into 12 equal sections and place them on the bread triangles. Sprinkle with thyme leaves.

Bake for 5-7 minutes on the top oven shelf. Drizzle with honey and serve immediately on top of the salad greens.

You can replace the tomatoes with cubes of pear or apple and walnuts.

Onion Tart

Annette Dure

This simple tart is delicious during the cold autumn and winter months.

Serves 8

Ingredients:

1 lb. 10 oz. peeled onions
1 1/2 Tbsp unsalted butter
1 egg yolk
3 heaping Tbsp crème fraîche
1/2 tsp salt, pinch of pepper
grated nutmeg to taste
1 express pastry crust **or**
   1 five grain cereal pastry
   shell (p. 56-57)
3/4 cup grated emmentaler or
   gruyère cheese (about 3 oz.)

1 Preheat the oven to 350°F. Peel and finely slice the onions. Put them in a pan with the melted butter. Brown them while stirring from time to time.

2 Lower the heat and cook for 20-30 minutes, stirring frequently. *The onions should have a beautiful golden color.*

3 Take the onions off the burner, and mix in the egg yolk and the fresh cream. Salt and pepper to taste. Add the grated nutmeg.

4 Pour the mixture into the crust in a 10 inch quiche dish. Sprinkle with the grated cheese. Bake for 30 minutes on the middle shelf of the oven.

Five Grain Cereal Mix Pastry Shell

Fanette Morice

This original pastry shell is a nice healthy change from other pastry crusts.

Ingredients for 1 pastry shell:

3/4 cup + 2 Tbsp water
1 cup five grain hot cereal mix
1 cup all purpose flour
6 Tbsp olive oil
1/4 tsp salt

Heat the water without bringing to a boil. Put the cereal mix in a bowl and pour the water over it to cover. Let the cereal swell up with the water for 5 minutes.

1 Put the saturated cereal grains, flour, oil, and salt together in a bowl.

2 Mix together with a fork.

3 Spread out the dough by hand in a 10 inch quiche dish. Pre-bake the crust for 15-20 minutes at 350°F. before garnishing. Once filled, bake again another 20 to 30 minutes. Bake the tart on the bottom shelf so the crust will become golden brown.

This shell is excellent for any savory tart. It is also a great alternative pastry for apple pies or other sweet tarts.

If making a sweet tart, omit the salt and add a Tbsp of honey to the mixture.

Express Pastry Crust

Agnès Delpuech

This time saving pastry crust recipe is a classic. You'll never hesitate to make another tart. Everyone loves it, including the cook!

Ingredients for 1 crust:

1 3/4 cups all purpose flour
1/2 tsp baking powder
5 1/3 Tbsp (1/3 cup) regular butter, melted **or** 1/3 cup oil
1/3 cup boiling water

Note: For a sweet tart, use unsalted butter and add one Tbsp sugar along with the baking powder and flour.

Put the flour and the baking powder into an airtight plastic bowl with a very tight fitting lid and shake.

1 Add the oil or the melted butter to the bowl. Add the boiling water. *Quickly* close the lid *securely* and shake vigorously while holding the lid tightly in place.

2 Make a ball of the dough and place it on a floured surface.

3 Roll out the dough with a rolling pin to the desired diameter and place it in a quiche dish or a pie pan.

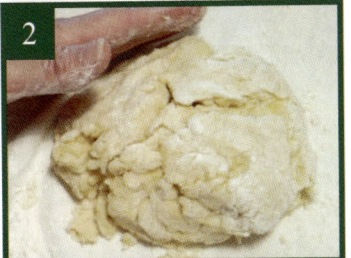

Tuna, Tomato, and Mozzarella Tart

Catherine Aramendy

Everyone loves this classic tart. It's easy and delicious.

Serves 6-8

Ingredients:

1 express pastry crust (see page 57)
1 Tbsp Dijon mustard
1 very heaping Tbsp bread crumbs
1 can tuna (5 oz.)
2-3 ripe but firm large tomatoes
1 ball fresh mozzarella (about 4-6 oz.)
garlic powder to taste
pinch of pepper
thyme leaves to taste
1 Tbsp olive oil
handful grated emmentaler or gruyère cheese

Preheat oven to 390°F. Line a quiche dish with parchment paper. Place the pastry crust on top.

1 Brush the mustard on the bottom of the crust, then evenly sprinkle the bread crumbs over top.

Drain the tuna and spread it over the bottom of the tart.

2 Cut the tomatoes into slices and lay them on top of the tuna.

Cut the fresh mozzarella into slices and alternate them with the tomato slices.

3 Sprinkle on the garlic powder, pepper, thyme leaves, and drizzle the olive oil over the top.

4 Sprinkle a little grated cheese on top.

Bake at 350°-390° F. for 30 minutes or more depending on your oven. Bon appétit!

> The breadcrumbs help absorb excess liquid from the tomatoes so the bottom crust bakes better. For sweet pastry tarts, you can sprinkle on some finely ground almonds instead of the breadcrumbs.

> 👨‍🍳 *You can try replacing the mozzarella with some cream cheese for a creamier texture.*

A Fun Variation for the Kids

Kimberly Sauvage

For 8 children: Follow the same directions as in the recipe on the opposite page, replacing the pastry crust with 4 hamburger buns. You will only need one tomato slice and one mozzarella slice per bun half. Open the buns side by side and place them on a baking sheet. Layer with the same ingredients that are in the tomato tart, maybe leaving out some herbs if the child does not like them. Bake at 350°F. for about 25 minutes. With a little less baking time and more "kid appeal," it's sure to please the cook as well as the kids.

For about 18 turnovers

Coca
(Red Pepper Turnovers)

Viviane Delpuech

Invite authentic North African flavors to your table with this delicious appetizer. They are also very good served cold on a picnic.

Ingredients:

4 red bell peppers (6 oz. each)
1 lb. small tomatoes
   (about 4)
3 medium sized red onions
   (11 1/2 oz.)
2 garlic cloves
3 Tbsp olive oil
1 tsp salt
pinch of pepper to taste
pinch of Cayenne pepper
double the express pastry
   crust recipe (see p. 57)

Place the peppers in the oven under the broiler for about 20 minutes. Turn them over from time to time. (See p.75) Let the peppers cool down under a dish towel.

1 Peel off the skin and take out the seeds by passing them very quickly under running water. Then cut them into strips.

2 Peel the tomatoes, cut them in half, take out the seeds, then cut them into large chunks.

3 Peel and cut the onions. Peel the garlic cloves and squeeze them through a garlic press.

Heat the oil in a pan. Add the onions and the garlic. Lightly brown on low heat.

4 Add the peppers and the tomatoes and cook on medium/high heat.

Salt and pepper to taste along with the Cayenne pepper and let cook for about 20 minutes or until all of the water evaporates. Stir often.

Put it in a colander with a bowl underneath. Let cool, then refrigerate all night so that it will be very well drained and cold *before garnishing the pastry crusts.*

The next day, preheat oven to 390° F.

5. Roll out the pastry dough. Cut out circles using a small 5 inch diameter bowl as a pattern.

6. Garnish each circle with about 1 Tbsp of the onions and peppers and tomatoes.

7. Fold the circles in half and pinch the edges together. Bake for about 30 minutes.

> 👨‍🍳 *You could replace the express pastry crust with puff pastry if you wish.*

> 👨‍🍳 *You can make one large tart with the same quantities in the ingredient list. In this case, you will only need to make one pastry crust.*

Carrot, Zucchini, and Cumin Puff Pastry Tart

Brigitte Kalms

This delicious vegetable tart stands in a class of its own because of its surprising cumin spice.

Serves 8

Ingredients:

1 lb. carrots (about 10 small/medium sized carrots)
7-8 Tbsp olive oil
3 heaping tsp cumin grains
2 lbs. zucchini squash (about 2-3 large zucchini)
2 eggs
1 tsp grated nutmeg
1 tsp salt
pinch of white pepper
3/4 cup heavy whipping cream
1 sheet puff pastry
1/2 cup grated emmentaler, gruyère, or parmesan cheese

Peel and cut the carrots into thin slices.

1 In a pan, lightly brown the carrots in 4 Tbsp olive oil on high heat.

Turn down to low heat and cook uncovered for about 20 minutes, stirring frequently. Add the cumin grains and cook for about 3-4 minutes longer. Set aside in a large bowl.

2 While cooking the carrots, peel the zucchini, cut in fourths lengthwise, then into small chunks.

In the same pan, add 3-4 more Tbsp olive oil and the zucchini. Cook very gently for about 25 minutes.

Preheat the oven (preferably a convection oven) to 390° F.

3 Pour the cooked zucchini into the same bowl as the carrots and add 1 egg. Mix well. Add the second egg and mix again.

4 Season with the nutmeg, salt, pepper, and add the cream. Gently mix together.

5 Either place the puff pastry sheet in a 9 inch pie pan lined with parchment paper, or gently roll it out to fit a 10 inch lined quiche pan. Prick the dough with a fork, then

pour the zucchini and carrot mixture into the pan. Sprinkle some of the grated cheese on top and bake for about 45 minutes.

Halfway through baking, add the rest of the grated cheese. Turn the pan around to ensure even baking.

This tart can be served accompanied by a green salad.

> *You might have to bake the tart longer in a traditional oven depending on the type of pan you use (glass, ceramic, etc.).*

> *Add the whipping cream little by little. If the mixture seems too liquid, you might not want to add quite all of the whipping cream.*

Cheese Soufflé

Jean François Dure

Here is an appetizing French classic that the whole family will love.

Serves 4

Ingredients for the Mornay sauce:

3 Tbsp unsalted butter
3 Tbsp flour
1 cup milk
1/2 tsp salt, pinch of pepper, ground nutmeg to taste
3 egg yolks
1 1/2 cup grated emmentaler or gruyère cheese

Ingredients for the soufflé:
5 egg whites

Preheat a convection oven to 390° F.

The Mornay Sauce:

1 Melt the butter in a pan. Add the flour and mix together with a whisk to make a roux. Let cook for 1-2 minutes before removing from the burner. Cool the pan in cold water in the sink.

2 Heat the milk in another pan. Pour the hot milk into the cooled roux and mix together. Bring it to a boil before turning off the heat. The rest of the recipe is off the burner.

3 Add salt, pepper, and grated nutmeg to taste. Add the three egg yolks to the sauce and mix with a whisk. Add the grated cheese and mix together to finish the sauce.

For the Soufflé:

4 Butter and lightly flour the entire surface of the inside of a soufflé dish (about 6 1/2" diameter by 3 1/2" deep) or any high walled pan that is suitable for the oven. Tap on the sides of the pan to remove any excess flour.

5 In a separate bowl, beat the egg whites along with a pinch of salt until peaks form. *This will take a few minutes.*

6 Fold in two large spoonfuls of egg whites into the Mornay sauce. Don't stir, fold them in very gently. Then gently incorporate the rest of the egg whites.

7 Fill the soufflé dish about 2/3 full. You can also put 4 thin slices of gruyère on the top for decoration.

8 Bake on the bottom rack of the oven for 25-30 minutes. When the top is golden brown and no longer jiggles, serve *immediately* right from the pan. It will "fall" fast!

The Soufflé

The Mornay Sauce

French Regional Cooking

France's 22 metropolitan regions boast as many culinary differences as its ever changing countryside. Indeed, each region's cuisine is greatly influenced by its geographical location. Brittany, a region bordering the sea, features many seafood dishes. Recipes from Normandy are famous for using butter and cream due to the region's superb dairy industry. Sun-ripened fruits and fresh vegetables, such as tomatoes, red peppers, olives, and garlic, are characteristic of dishes originating from the Mediterranean's culinary regions such as Provence and Rousillon.

Take a culinary tour and experience the art of French regional cooking starting in our own Spanish-influenced French Catalonia. Then travel with us to southern Provence, world renowned for its lavender fields and herbs. Stop with us in the Rhône Valley and Auvergne before traveling northeast to Lorraine and the picturesque Vosges Mountains in Alsace. Finish your journey of the rich culinary heritage of France in the famous northern beaches of Normandy.

Catalan Chicken

Sylvia Garcia

This simmered, hearty main dish from the French Catalonia is appreciated by all.

Serves 4-6

Ingredients:

2 1/2 red bell peppers (1 lb.)
4 medium onions
6 chicken pieces
    (about 12 oz.)
2 Tbsp olive oil
3 tsp dried thyme leaves
salt and pepper to taste
    (or about 1/2 tsp each)
1 can (28 oz.) peeled whole
    tomatoes (3 3/4 cups)
2 tsp sugar

1 Cut the peppers into thin strips. Cut the onions in half then into thin slices.

2 Heat the olive oil in a high sided pan. Brown all sides of the chicken in the olive oil with the thyme leaves. Salt and pepper to taste. Set aside the chicken in another dish.

3 Brown the peppers in the same pan for about 10 minutes on medium heat. Add a little oil if necessary.

4 Add the onions and stir.

5 Return the browned chicken to the pan along with the can of peeled tomatoes. Add the sugar and stir together.

Cook uncovered on reduced heat for at least 45 minutes.

> This Catalan sauce is also typically cooked with rabbit, snails, or cod fish.

> For a spicier sauce, add a few drops of Tabasco.

You can gently simmer for a longer period of time to bring out the full flavors.

Serve with potatoes or rice.

"Ja que Déu ha estimat tant el món,
que ha donat el seu Fill únic
perquè tot el qui creu en ell no es perdi,
sinó que tingui vida eterna."

John 3:16 in Catalan

"For God so loved the world,
that he gave his only begotten Son,
that whosoever believeth in Him should not perish,
but have everlasting life."

John 3:16

Boles de Picoulat
Catalan Meatballs

Raymonde Boëls

This typical Catalan dish with its delicious meatballs in a mildly spicy olive sauce makes a very inviting meal.

Serves 8 (25-30 meatballs)

Ingredients for the meatballs:

3 large garlic cloves and several full parsley sprigs
14 oz. sausage
14 oz. ground beef
3 eggs
1 cup all purpose flour
3 Tbsp olive oil

Ingredients for the sauce:

1 small handful dried porcini mushrooms (1/2 oz.)
2 small onions (about 5 oz.)
2 Tbsp sunflower oil and 1 Tbsp butter
6-7 oz. bacon, cut in pieces
1 cup pitted green olives
1 can (14 oz.) mushroom slices or whole button mushrooms
1 heaping Tbsp double concentrated tomato paste
3 Tbsp all purpose flour
1 can (14 oz.) whole peeled tomatoes (1 1/2 cup)
2 tsp sugar with 1 tsp vinegar
1 bouillon cube, chicken or beef (dissolved in 1 cup water)
2 dried bay leaves
1 tsp dried thyme leaves
1 can (28 oz.) white beans (3 cups, optional)

1 Put the dried porcini mushrooms in a small bowl. Cover with water (about 2/3 cup).

Meatballs: Chop together the garlic cloves and the parsley leaves. There should be around 5 heaping Tbsp. Set aside.

Put the sausage and the ground beef in a large bowl. Season with 1 tsp salt and a pinch of pepper. Add the eggs and the chopped garlic and parsley. Mix well.

2 Put the cup of flour on a plate. Make the meatballs with your hands or with the help of 2 spoons, then roll them in the flour.

3 Heat the olive oil in a pan and brown the outside of the meatballs.

Sauce: Chop the onions with a food processor.

Heat the sunflower oil and butter in another large pot.

Add the chopped onions

along with the bacon cut into small pieces. Cook on medium heat.

4 Add the olives, the drained button mushrooms and the porcini mushrooms. (*Save the water from the porcini mushrooms for later!*) Mix together. Add the tomato paste, 3 Tbsp flour, and mix again.

5 Add the can of tomatoes and the water from the porcini mushrooms along with the 2 tsp sugar soaked with 1 tsp vinegar. Stir.

6 Dissolve the bouillon cube in 1 cup water and add it to the pot. Stir. Add 1/2 tsp salt and a pinch of pepper to taste. Add the bay leaves and the thyme leaves.

Put the browned meatballs back into the sauce and let simmer covered for about 10-15 minutes until the meatballs are cooked through. Stir often to prevent sticking! Add the white beans before serving.

> *This is an ideal dish to reheat the next day.*

Note: Spanish cooking uses a lot of oil. Oil amounts can be reduced if preferred.

Ratatouille

French Vegetable Stew

Cathy Scotto

Here is one of the many variations of the classic Provençal savory stew that can be eaten warm, hot, or even cold.

Ingredients for 8-10 servings:

- 5 red peppers (about 6 oz. each)
- 3 eggplants (about 12 oz. each)
- 6 small zucchini (7 oz. each)
- 10 firm tomatoes (4 1/2 lbs)
- 6 large garlic cloves
- 1/4 cup olive oil
- 1-2 cups unpitted black olives, according to taste
- 1 full cup pitted green olives
- 1 heaping tsp thyme leaves
- several sprigs fresh basil (optional)
- several sprigs parsley
- 5 fresh or dried bay leaves
- 1/2 tsp salt and 1 tsp pepper

Preparation: Roast the peppers under the broiler in order to peel them. (see opposite page)

1 While keeping a watchful eye on the peppers, peel the eggplants, zucchini, and tomatoes.

2 Cut the eggplants lengthwise into thin slices. Place them side by side on a large platter. Sprinkle salt on both sides allowing the salt to draw out the water. Set aside.

Cut the zucchini into thin slices lengthwise like the eggplants. Set aside.

3 Peel the tomatoes. Cut them in half horizontally and remove the seeds. Place them upside down in a colander to drain any excess juice.

4 Cut the tomatoes into cubes and set aside.

5 Peel and remove the seeds from the roasted peppers. Cut them into strips and set aside.

Cut the garlic cloves in half and remove the center sprout. Set aside.

> According to certain French cooks, to avoid garlic odor on your hands after handling garlic, rub your fingers on the flat side of a stainless steel knife under cold running water.

How to Peel Red Peppers

Place the peppers under the broiler for about 20 minutes. Turn them over from time to time.

1. Leave them until their skin becomes black.
2. Once cooled, their skin comes off very easily by rubbing them between your fingers.
3. Pull on both ends to remove the stem and the seeds.

Cooking:

Heat some olive oil in a pan, or several pans in order to save time. Non-stick pans will need less oil. Note that 1/4 cup olive oil should be enough to brown all of the vegetables in a nonstick pan.

6 Lightly brown the zucchini on medium heat, turning them over from time to time. Add more olive oil a little at a time. The pan should not be dry. *Be careful to drizzle the oil onto the pan and not on the vegetables.* The zucchini should turn golden brown.

Wipe the eggplants with a paper towel or a dish towel to absorb the moisture. Brown the eggplants the same as the zucchini.

7 Brown the peppers very rapidly while stirring, just enough to evaporate the water.

8 *After browning each vegetable, add it to a large pot or pressure cooker.*

Proceed with the tomatoes the same way as the peppers to evaporate some water.

Lightly brown the garlic cloves and add them to the vegetables in the pot.

9 Add the black and green olives and the thyme leaves.

10 Finely chop the basil leaves, parsley, and bay leaves and add them also. Salt and pepper to taste.

Stir very gently without crushing the vegetables. Taste and adjust the seasoning if necessary.

Cover and let simmer for at least 45 minutes to 1 hour. Or you can pressure cook it for 30-45 minutes. You may want to gently simmer a little longer uncovered to fully bring out the flavors.

> *This dish can be served with couscous, meat kebobs, or simply with fried eggs and bread.*

> *The ingredient list gives approximate ounces for certain vegetables and serves as a "base recipe." Feel free to use slightly more or less quantity depending on the size of the vegetables.*

> A fast way to peel ripe tomatoes is to first rub the whole surface of the tomato skin with the sharp side of a knife blade. The skin will then peel off with little effort.

Did You Know

According to certain cooks, you can prevent garlic breath by taking out the center sprout of the garlic clove, which also makes it easier to digest.

"Thy Word is truth."
John 17:17

The Best from the Rest

Ratatouille and Tuna Tart

Fanette Morice

This tart made from leftover Ratatouille is fast and delicious.

Serves 8

Ingredients:

1 homemade express pastry crust (p. 57)
2 1/2 cups leftover ratatouille
1 can (5 oz.) tuna in water
1/2 cup crème fraîche, fresh cream
salt and pepper to taste
1-2 tsp thyme leaves to taste
grated emmentaler or gruyère cheese

1 Add this mixture to the ratatouille, stir, and let cook for 5 minutes on low heat. To keep the crust from becoming soggy, slightly drain the ratatouille mixture before pouring onto the crust.

2 Sprinkle with grated cheese. Bake for 25-30 minutes at 410°F.

Roll out the pastry dough to fit a 10 inch quiche dish and prick the surface of the bottom of the shell with the prongs of a fork. Bake in the oven for 5 minutes at 410°F.

Cook the ratatouille leftovers in a pan in order to evaporate any water. In the meantime, drain the tuna and mix it with the fresh cream in a bowl. Add salt, pepper, and thyme leaves to taste.

Gratin Dauphinois
Potatoes au Gratin

Cathy Scotto

This simple potato dish from the Dauphiné region is the most heavenly way to eat potatoes.

Serves 6-8

Ingredients:

4 1/2 lbs. potatoes
2 cups heavy whipping cream
1/2 cup milk
3 level Tbsp garlic powder
2 tsp salt, 1/2 tsp pepper
1/2 tsp grated nutmeg
1 1/2 Tbsp and 1/2 Tbsp unsalted butter
1 garlic clove

Preheat oven to 340°F.

Peel the potatoes and thinly slice them by hand or in the food processor.

1 Put them in a large bowl with all of the ingredients except the garlic clove and butter.

2 Mix well. (It is more practical with your hands.) The cream and milk will be about the same level as the potatoes in the bowl.

3 Grease a 9 x 13 inch glass dish with 1/2 Tbsp butter. Cut the garlic clove in half and rub it all over the bottom of the dish. Then finely dice the garlic clove and spread it over the bottom surface of the dish.

Pour the potatoes into the dish. Cut the 1 1/2 Tbsp butter into small pieces and place them on top. Bake for 1 1/2 hours at 340° F.

Gratin Savoyard

Jaqueline Franco

These savory mashed potatoes from Savoie in the Rhône Alpes are the perfect accompaniment for that special Sunday dinner.

Serves 8

Ingredients:

3 lbs. potatoes

2 large onions (about 14 oz.)

2-3 shallots, makes 1/2 cup chopped (about 2 1/2 oz.)

7 oz. bacon slices

2 Tbsp butter

2 cups milk

2 Tbsp all purpose flour

1 tsp salt

1/2 tsp pepper

3 eggs, beaten

4 full parsley sprigs

2 cups shredded emmentaler or gruyère cheese (6 oz.)

Boil the unpeeled potatoes in water until very tender. This could take from 25-45 minutes, depending on the potato size. Let cool slightly.

Preheat oven to 460 °F.

1 During this time, peel and chop the onions and the shallots.

2 Cut the bacon strips into small pieces.

Melt the butter in a pan. Add the onions and shallots.

3 Lightly brown them on medium heat for about 2 minutes. Lower the heat and add the bacon pieces. Cook for another 5-7 minutes.

Peel the cooled potatoes and mash them with a fork in a large mixing bowl.

4 Stir the milk into the potatoes.

5 Add the flour, salt, pepper, and beaten eggs to the potatoes. Mix well.

6 Add the onions, shallots, and bacon pieces. Stir again.

7 Cut the parsley sprigs with scissors and mix

them into the potatoes along with the grated cheese.

Pour into a 9 x 13 inch dish. Bake at 460° F for about 35 minutes. The top will become a beautiful golden brown.

If you would like a smoother texture, you could mash the potatoes with an electric mixer instead of with a fork.

Stuffed Cabbage

Cathy Scotto

This typical dish from the Auvergne region is as savory as it is spectacular.

Serves 6

Ingredients :
1 large Savoy cabbage
1 3/4 oz. bread (about 1 1/2 slices of bread)
1/3 cup milk
14- 17 oz. sausage
2 Tbsp and 2 Tbsp olive oil
5 garlic cloves
1 small handful parsley leaves, (about 1/3 cup)
1 Tbsp all purpose flour
1 egg
20 pitted green olives (1/2 cup)
1 heaping tsp dried thyme leaves
1/2 tsp salt, pinch of pepper
kitchen string
1 bouillon cube dissolved in 1/2 cup water

Bring a little over 3 quarts water, about 13 1/2 cups, to boil in a large pot. Put the cabbage in and cook for about 20 minutes in order to blanch it.

1. Stop cooking when you can easily separate the leaves with a knife.

Drain it in a colander, and set it aside to cool. Place the cooled cabbage on a large, clean kitchen towel that you will also use later in the recipe.

Soak the bread in milk.

To make the stuffing, brown the sausage in a pan with 2 Tbsp of olive oil.

2. Chop the garlic cloves and the parsley leaves separately and add them to the browned sausage.

3 Turn off the heat and add the soaked bread, flour, and egg to the stuffing.

4 Chop the olives into pieces and put them in as well. Add the thyme leaves, salt, and pepper.

Mix well and let the stuffing sit for about 10 minutes.

Gently separate the cabbage leaves, working your way almost all the way to the center.

5 Insert about one spoonful of the stuffing all the way around the cabbage's center.

6 Working towards the outside leaves, fold up one layer of leaves at a time, making sure to put stuffing in between the leaves.

7 Fold up the opposite corners of the towel and tie a knot. Tighten hard in order to give the cabbage a nice shape.

8 Take off the towel and wrap kitchen string around the cabbage several times so that it will hold together well.

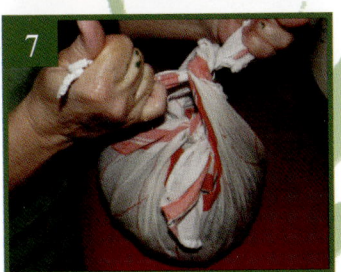

Put the stuffed cabbage in a pressure cooker along with the other 2 Tbsp olive oil.

9 Dissolve the bouillon cube in about 1/2 cup water. Add it to the pressure cooker along with 1 1/2 more cups water. Cover and cook for 45 minutes after the pressure is reached. *(The time could be longer depending on the size of the cabbage.) It is cooked when you can easily thrust a knife into its center.*

10 To serve, cut the cabbage as if you were cutting a round cake.

Stuffed cabbage is usually accompanied by rice or potatoes.

Variation

Cabbage Gratin

Annette Dure

If you don't have time to make the stuffed cabbage, here is a similar recipe under a different form, gratin style.

Cut the cabbage into fourths and blanch it for 20 minutes. Drain. Prepare the stuffing for the cabbage in the same manner as the other recipe with the following ingredients:

some bread soaked in warm water then gently squeezed,
17 oz. sausage,
1 garlic clove,
1 chopped onion,
3 eggs,
1 small handful chopped parsley leaves, and salt and pepper.

Mix together. Cut the cabbage into pieces and spread half of it in the bottom of a large dish. Spread the stuffing in a layer on top of the cabbage and finish with a top layer of the remaining cabbage. Spread some grated emmentaler or gruyère cheese on top and bake in the oven at 320°F. for 45 minutes to 1 hour. Serve in the dish.

Quiche Lorraine

Fanette Morice

This classic quiche from the Lorraine region is simple and versatile to fit anyone's taste.

Ingredients for 8 servings:

1 express pastry crust, see p. 57, *or* 1 puff pastry
7 oz. bacon slices
3 eggs
1 cup milk
1/4 cup heavy whipping cream or crème fraîche (fresh cream)
1/8 tsp pepper
1/4 tsp ground nutmeg

Prepare the pastry crust in a 10 inch quiche dish and preheat the oven to 350°F.

1 Cut the bacon slices into pieces. Cook the bacon pieces on medium heat for about 5 minutes.

2 Whisk together the eggs, milk, and cream. Stir in the pepper and nutmeg. Do not salt.

3 Spread the bacon pieces evenly over the bottom of the crust before pouring the egg mixture on top.

Bake for 30 minutes at 350° F. on a rack in the lower half of the oven. Serve warm or cooled.

You can add shredded cheese on top before baking. Some replace the bacon with ham or salmon and add 2-3 small leeks sautéed in 2-3 Tbsp butter.

Munster Valley Pie

Brigitte Kalms

This traditional minced meat pie is served in all the country inns of the Vosges Mountains during the early winter months.

Serves 6-8

Ingredients:

- 2 1/4 oz. bread, about two slices, soaked in about 3/4 cup cream or milk
- 2 medium sized onions (about 1 3/4 cups chopped)
- 5 Tbsp unsalted butter
- 2 lb. ground pork (neck or shoulder)
- 2 eggs
- 1/3 cup packed minced parsley
- 3 garlic cloves
- 1/2 tsp ground cloves
- 1 tsp ground nutmeg
- 1 tsp salt, 1/2 tsp pepper
- 2 sheets puff pastry, thawed
- 1 egg, separated

Soak the bread in the milk. Mash the bread with a fork.

1 Chop the onions into small pieces.

2 Brown them lightly in the butter.

Preheat the oven, preferably a convection oven, to 390°F.

Put the ground pork in a large bowl. Stir in the browned onions, 2 eggs, and the soaked bread.

3 Add the minced parsley, pressed garlic cloves, ground cloves, nutmeg, salt and pepper, and mix well.

Roll out one sheet of puff pastry in a 10 inch large circle on parchment paper. Place the parchment paper on a large baking sheet with sides (at least 10 inches wide). You can grease the pan with butter before laying down the parchment paper to prevent it from slipping if you wish.

4 Form the meat mixture as a high dome on the puff pastry. Fold up the puff pastry around the meat dome.

5 Rub the sides of the pastry with a cotton pad (or a brush) dipped in egg white. This will help seal the top crust with the bottom crust.

6 Gently roll out the other pastry sheet slightly larger (about 11-12 inches in diameter). Cover the meat and tuck the sides in underneath the bottom crust.

7 As decoration, you can lightly run a knife over the top of the pastry to create small lines. Just be very careful not to actually cut through the pastry dough. Brush the top lightly with the egg yolk to give it a nice golden brown color.

Bake for about 1 hour at 390°F. Turn the baking sheet around after one half hour of baking. This pie is often served with a green salad.

> *If possible, make the pork mixture the night before.*

Normandy Chicken

Jacqueline Franco

This savory dish from Normandy with its generous fresh cream sauce is very appealing.

Serves 6

Ingredients for the chicken:

2 carrots (around 7 oz.)
2 large onions (6-7 oz. each)
2 full parsley sprigs
5 Tbsp unsalted butter
1 large chicken (3-4 lbs.)
1 Tbsp salt and 1 tsp pepper

Ingredients for the sauce:

11 oz. fresh button mushrooms
1/2 tsp salt and pinch of pepper
juice from 1/2 lemon
2 Tbsp and 5 Tbsp unsalted butter
5 Tbsp all purpose flour
4 egg yolks
1 cup crème fraîche (fresh cream)

Peel and cut the carrots and the onion into slices. Roughly chop the parsley into pieces.

1 Using a very large deep pot, lightly brown the sliced carrots, onion, and parsley in butter.

Place the chicken on top of the vegetables.

2 Cover the chicken entirely with water.

Salt and pepper to taste.

Bring to a boil and let simmer on low heat for about 1 hour.

The Sauce: Prepare the sauce towards the end of the cooking time for the chicken.

3 Wash and slice the mushrooms. Put them in a small saucepan with 3 cups cold water, 1/2 tsp salt, a pinch of pepper, the lemon juice, and 2 Tbsp butter. Cover and gently boil for 5 minutes, then turn off the burner.

4 During this time, melt the remaining butter (5 Tbsp) in another sauce pan. Make a **roux** by adding the flour to the melted butter.

The roux

Take out 2 cups broth from the cooked chicken. Slowly pour it on top of the roux while stirring with a wire whisk. This is the **sauce**.

5 Add 3/4 cup of the cooking water from the mushrooms to this sauce and cook for 15 minutes.

The sauce

6 *Tempering the Eggs:* Mix the egg yolks with the fresh cream in a small bowl. Slowly add 1/2 cup cooking water from the mushrooms while stirring. Add a small ladleful of the sauce and gently whisk it in with the egg mixture as well.

Tempering the eggs

7 Pour these tempered eggs back into the sauce. Briefly boil, then remove from heat, but keep the sauce warm.

Cut the chicken and arrange the chicken pieces on a serving dish. Drain the mushrooms and place around the chicken. Coat the chicken with some of the sauce. Serve the remaining sauce over rice.

Leftover chicken broth can be made into a soup.

Add the tempered eggs to the sauce

Dishes from Around the World

Pineapple Pork

Jean Marc Sauvage

This flavorful dish has a very colorful presentation.

Ingredients for 4-6 servings:

6 pork steaks (about 2 lbs. with bone)
1/2 yellow or green bell pepper
1/2 red bell pepper
1 small white or red onion (4 oz.)
1 red chili pepper (optional)
1/2 fresh large pineapple
2 large garlic cloves
3 Tbsp oil
6 Tbsp soy sauce
salt and pepper
4 heaping Tbsp sugar

1 **Preparation:** Cut the pork into about 1 1/4 inch cubes.

2 Open, seed, and cut the peppers into slices, then small sticks (1/2 cup each).

3 Slice the onion, then cut the slices in half. Seed the chili pepper and cut it into tiny cubes (1 tsp).

4 Cut off the top of the pineapple and take out the fruit with a knife and a soup spoon. Save the hollow rind. Cut half of the pineapple fruit into medium size cubes (about 1 1/2 cups).

Peel the garlic cloves, take out the center sprout, and chop them very finely.

5 **Cooking:** Heat 2 Tbsp of oil in a pan to around 350°F. (When small bubbles form around a wooden spoon in contact with the hot oil you know you have reached the right temperature.) Add the onions and garlic. Lightly brown them.

6 Add 2 Tbsp soy sauce and the peppers. Add a little salt and pepper. Lower heat slightly and cook so the peppers become crisp but tender. If it starts sticking to the pan, add 1-2 Tbsp water. Take off heat after about 7 minutes. Set aside.

Add the other Tbsp oil to the pan and the cubes of pork with 4 Tbsp soy sauce. Cover, and cook for 10 minutes.

7 Uncover and add the drained pineapple cubes and the chili pepper. Spread them out but do not mix them with the pork.

Preparation: *Cooking:*

Wait one minute, then put the other vegetables back in the pan and stir together.

8 Turn off the heat. Make the caramel. (See page 95) Add it right away to the pork. Cook the pineapple pork with the caramel for another 5 minutes. Serve with rice.

> 👨‍🍳 You could replace fresh pineapple with canned pineapple.

> 👨‍🍳 We recommend cooking your rice in a rice cooker.

The Best from the Rest

Thailand-Style Rice

This easy, flavorful, and colorful rice is the perfect accompaniment to the pineapple pork, but is also excellent by itself. It's also a great way to use the other half of the fresh pineapple.

Ingredients for 4-6:

small bunch (5-6 small stems) green onions (1/4 cup cut)
1/2 fresh pineapple or canned (about 1 1/2 cups diced)
3-4 links of Chinese pork sausage (Asian market)
1-2 Tbsp oil, depending on the leanness of the sausage
1 tsp turmeric powder
5 cups cooked jasmine or basmati rice (in a rice cooker)

1 Chop the green stems from the bunch of onions.

2 Cut the pineapple half and the sausages into small pieces.

3 Heat the oil in a nonstick pan, then add the onions. A few seconds later, add and brown the sausage.

4 Add the pineapple and the turmeric. Stir in the cooked rice and let it fry for about 2 minutes. Filling the empty pineapple rind with rice makes a spectacular centerpiece.

> 🧑‍🍳 You can use the onion part of the green onions with the other onions in the pineapple pork if you wish.

The Caramel for the Pineapple Pork :

Put 4 heaping Tbsp sugar in a saucepan.

The sugar will brown rapidly.

Let melt on high heat.

Immediately pour in about 3/4 cup water and stir. **Be careful! Stand back when pouring! It's going to splatter.**

Sautéed Vegetables in Oyster Sauce

Jean Marc Sauvage

These al dente vegetables sautéed in a tasty oyster sauce are bright and colorful.

Serves 4-6

Ingredients:

1 small handful dried black fungus (about 1/2 oz.)
4 small carrots (8 1/2 oz.)
1 red bell pepper (6 oz.)
1 green bell pepper (6 oz.)
1 broccoli head (around 1 lb.)
1 small red onion (4 oz.)
6 garlic cloves
1 small tomato (4 oz., *optional*)
1 head Chinese cabbage (2 lbs.)
1 Tbsp fish sauce (nuoc mam)
3 Tbsp oil
2 Tbsp soy sauce
salt and pepper
4 heaping Tbsp oyster sauce (according to taste), *foreign food aisle of grocery store*
1 small can young corn pieces (*optional*)

Preparation:

Let the black fungus soak for 30 minutes in a bowl of hot water.

Cut the carrots into small sticks and cut the peppers into small slices.

Cut the broccoli florets off the head of broccoli.

Cut the onion into small slices and the garlic clove into very small pieces.

Cut the tomato into half moon shapes. Cut off the end of the cabbage as well as some of the hard center. Cut the rest of the cabbage (about 1 1/2 lb.) into pieces.

Finally, drain and cut the fungus into slices.

You could wash and cut the vegetables the day before and put them in the refrigerator. You could even cook the carrots, peppers, and broccoli al dente the day before and refrigerate. Last minute cooking will be easier and quicker when guests are present.

Preparation

Chinese cabbage is widely used in cooking. It can be used raw in salads or added at the end of cooking as is the case in some Asian dishes.

Cooking: Boil a pot of water with the fish sauce.

1. When the water boils, add the carrots, peppers, and broccoli. You need to cook them *al dente* (rolling boil for about 3 minutes). When the dull side of a knife barely cuts through the vegetables, take the pan off the heat. ***Pour the vegetables immediately into a colander to drain and run them under cold water to stop the cooking process.***

2. Heat the oil in a pan to about 350°F. (When small bubbles form around a wooden spoon in contact with the hot oil, you know you have reached the right temperature.) Lightly brown the garlic and the onions for a minute on medium heat. Add the soy sauce. Salt (only a little!) and pepper (about 1/2 tsp).

3. Add all the pieces of cabbage, then the oyster sauce according to your taste and mix it well. Let cook on medium to medium/high heat for about 10 minutes. The cabbage will decrease greatly in volume while cooking.

4. Add the drained black fungus along with the cooked carrots, peppers, and broccoli. Stir together. Let cook for another minute, then add the tomatoes and the baby corn. Serve with rice cooked in a rice cooker.

You could use salt instead of fish sauce in the cooking water.

These vegetables nicely accompany a steak.

Pork Spring Rolls

Esther Sephanh

This southeast Vietnamese specialty has so much more flavor than the store bought counterpart.

Makes 15-20 spring rolls

Ingredients:

1 3/4 oz. bean thread
    vermicelli (oriental noodles)
handful black fungus (about
    1/2 oz.)
1 medium sized onion
    (4 1/2 oz.)
1 medium sized potato (6 oz.)
1 medium sized carrot (3 oz.)
7-7 1/2 oz. lean pork steak
    (or chicken)
1/2 tsp salt and pepper
3 Tbsp soy sauce
1 Tbsp fish sauce (nuoc mam)
1 package rice wrappers
    (8.5 inch standard size)
sunflower oil for frying
    (4 1/2-5 cups)

Filling Preparation:

Soak the vermicelli in 4 1/2 cups of very hot water for about 30 minutes.

Put the black fungus in very hot water also. Let them soak for 30 minutes as well.

Peel the onion, the potato, and the carrot.

1 Take the fat off the pork and cut the pork into about 3/8 inch cubes before grinding it in the food processor. Put the ground pork in a large, deep bowl.

2 Cut the onion and the potato into large cubes before grinding them as well. They need to be finely ground. Add them to the ground pork in the bowl.

3. Grate the carrot and add it to the bowl. Rinse and drain the black fungus before grinding. Put them in the bowl.

4. Add the salt, pepper, soy sauce, and fish sauce to the bowl and mix everything together well.

5. Drain the vermicelli and cut them up a little with scissors before adding them to the mixture in the bowl. Mix all the ingredients together well with your hands or a wooden spatula.

Put the oil in a wok or a *high sided pan* to heat while filling the rice wrappers.

Wet two large kitchen towels under running water. Wring them out and spread out one of the towels on a working surface.

6. Take one rice wrapper at a time and dip it in a pan of hot water for a few seconds.

7. Lay out 4-6 wrappers on the towel. Cover them with the other wet towel for several seconds and remove.

8. Put one Tbsp filling on the bottom of each wrapper.

9. Following the pictures, fold the bottom layer up over the filling, then fold

Rice Wrappers:

You can find these spring roll wrappers, also called rice paper, in the foreign food aisle of your larger supermarket or in your local Asian market.

You can replace the pork with ground chicken if you wish.

Assembly:

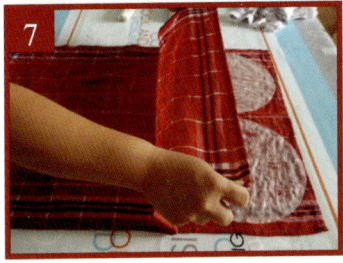

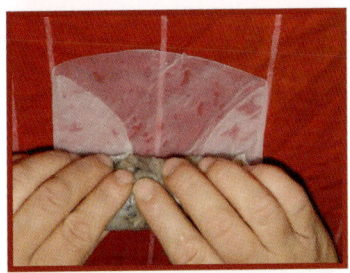

over both sides before **tightly** rolling it up to prevent air bubbles. Repeat with each wrapper. Put them in the slightly hot oil which *should only be hot enough to bubble gently around the spring rolls while cooking.*

10 Turn them over from time to time with metal tongs. After about 15 minutes, when the oil starts bubbling less, take them out and drain them on a paper towel for several seconds. You can eat them hot, warm, or even cold, dipped in a sweet and sour or spring roll sauce.

Although the oil should only be hot enough to gently boil, always be careful while frying and do not leave the oil unattended.

Colombo
Martinique-Style Curry Chicken

Jean Luc Thurard

This spicy authentic recipe from the West Indies traditionally served with rice makes a very hearty meal.

Serves 4

Ingredients:

- 9-11 oz. chicken breasts or chicken thighs
- 1 can (14 oz.) mushrooms
- 1 small jar pitted green olives, (reserve the juice)
- 1 tsp dried parsley
- 1 tsp dried chives
- 2 tsp dried thyme
- 1 tsp dried basil
- 1 tsp garlic powder
- 1 tsp shallot powder (or 1 chopped small shallot)
- 2 tsp salt
- 1 large lemon or lime
- 3 large potatoes
- 1 large onion (5 oz.)
- 3 Tbsp olive oil
- 1 1/2 oz. colombo spice powder (about 1/2 cup)

Marinade: Cut the chicken into large pieces. If using chicken thighs, take off the skin. Put them in a bowl that has an airtight lid.

1 Add the can of drained mushrooms, about 15 green olives, and 1/3 cup of the olive juice to the chicken.

2 Add all of the dried herbs. Salt and pepper to taste. Mix together.

3 Cut the lemon into slices and squeeze the juice over the chicken. Mix well with the chicken so that it is well saturated with the marinade.

Cover and refrigerate overnight.

Cooking the next day: Peel and cut the potatoes into fourths. Slice the onions.

4 In a large pot, brown the pieces of chicken in olive oil. Take them out and set aside.

5 Brown the onions in the same pot on low heat for about 10 minutes.

Add the potatoes and stir with a wooden spoon while cooking on low heat.

6 Add the reserved browned chicken and the rest of its marinade. You can cut the olives into fourths.

7 Add the colombo spice and stir. *(Feel free to add more colombo powder if you prefer spicy food. Colombo is traditionally made with almost 3 oz. colombo powder!)* Add just enough cold water to cover the contents of the pot.

> 👨‍🍳 *For a summer Colombo, you can put in several pieces of zucchini and eggplant. Just add them along with the potatoes in the recipe.*

Simmer for 20-45 minutes, or until the potatoes are well cooked. They should break up when you stick them with a fork. Add some water while cooking if needed. Serve hot with rice cooked with a chicken bouillon cube.

Gourmet Salad

Jean Marc Sauvage

This original, colorful salad, which changes according to the season, is always easy to make for family or guests.

Ingredients for 8:
2 small cantaloupe melons
1 large lettuce head
parsley leaves, *optional*
9 oz. Cantal cheese, or any cheddar or semi firm cheese
12 oz. Brie cheese
purple and green grapes
8 large slices specialty deli bread (French country, etc...)
8 slices prosciutto cured ham
7 oz. emmentaler cheese, grated (around 3 cups)
7 Tbsp cumin grains
balsamic vinaigrette (*found by other salad dressings*)

1 Cut the melons in half and scoop out the seeds with a spoon. Cut them into slices, following the green lines. Count 2 slices per plate. Cut the melon from its rind with a knife, cutting not quite to the other end. One end needs to stay attached.

2 Wash the lettuce and cut it into ribbon slices. Arrange it on some big plates with the melons. Sprinkle with some parsley leaves.

3 Cut the cheese into slices lengthwise and add it to the plates.

4 Wash the grapes and arrange them nicely on the plates. Drizzle the vinaigrette over the lettuce.

5 Lightly toast the bread slices in the toaster. Lay a slice of prosciutto on each bread slice.

6 Sprinkle a thick layer of grated emmentaler on each slice. Sprinkle them with the cumin grains.

7 Place under the broiler for about 5 minutes. Take out of the oven, and cut the bread into slices if you desire.

Serve the hot bread on the bed of salad.

Winter Variation

For a delicious, festive alternative, you could replace the grapes and the melon with grapefruit cut into quarters. Toast the bread, then let it cool. Spread a thick coat of crème fraîche (thick cream) on each slice of bread. Add a slice of smoked salmon and sprinkle with dill. Sprinkle some cranberries on the plate for decoration. It's delicious!

 You could prepare everything before the guests arrive, then put the bread under the broiler at the last minute.

Seafood Enchiladas

Kimberly Sauvage

This family recipe combines classic Mexican and seafood with a white cheese sauce.

Serves 4-6

Ingredients:

4 Tbsp (1/2 stick) regular butter or margarine
3 Tbsp flour
1 cup milk
1/2 tsp salt
1 lb. grated Monterrey Jack cheese
8 oz. small frozen cooked shrimp
8 oz. crab or imitation crab
1 package Chi Chi fiesta restaurante seasoning mix
10 six inch flour or corn tortillas
1 green onion sliced (optional)

Preheat oven to 350°F.

Melt the butter in a saucepan. Add the flour and salt. Stir.

1 Add the milk and stir until thickened.

2 Add 12 oz. of the grated cheese to the white sauce. Stir until smooth then turn off heat.

3 In a large bowl, mix together the thawed shrimp, chunks of crab, and seasoning.

4 Put one large spoonful of white cheese sauce on a tortilla.

5 Add a large spoonful of the shrimp and crab mixture and roll up the tortilla. Place it seam side down in a 9 x 12 inch dish.

Repeat the process with the remaining tortillas. You should have some white cheese sauce left.

6 Seal the edges of the rolled tortillas in the dish with some of the remaining sauce to keep them moist.

7 Pour what is left of the sauce over the top of all the tortillas.

8 Top with the remaining grated cheese and the sliced green onion for color.

Bake at 350° F. for 30 minutes until warmed completely through and the cheese on top is melted.

Top with hot or mild salsa. This is delicious accompanied by tortilla chips and our homemade guacamole dip (see p. 32).

If the tortillas tend to crack, microwave each one a few seconds before filling and rolling it.

Tandoori Chicken

Brigitte Kalms

This spiced chicken is delicious hot, warm, or cold. It's a wonderful idea for a barbecue or a picnic.

Serves 2-3

Ingredients:

1 lb. chicken pieces, preferably boneless (about 5 chicken thighs)
1/2 cup plain yogurt
2 Tbsp olive oil
2 Tbsp lemon juice (about half a lemon)
2 1/2 Tbsp Tandoori spice powder
1 tsp salt

Preparation the Day Before:

Everything must be prepared the day before.

1. Take off the skin, debone the thighs if needed, and cut the chicken into equal pieces.

2. Pour the yogurt into a mixing bowl. Add the olive oil and mix together with a wire whisk. Be careful not to beat it. Add the lemon juice, the Tandoori spice powder, and the salt.

3. Mix together with the wire whisk.

4. Place the chicken pieces in this marinade.

5. Cover the bowl with plastic wrap, being careful to place it directly over the chicken. Push the air pockets out carefully, then stick the plastic wrap to the sides of the bowl. Put it in the refrigerator overnight.

Baking the Next Day:

Preheat your oven, preferably a convection oven, to 460°F.

Take the marinade out of the refrigerator.

Completely cover the bottom of your broiler pan with aluminum foil.

6. Put the chicken pieces on the top of the broiler pan.

Bake for about 10-15 minutes. Turn them over, and bake again for another 10-15 minutes.

Serve with any variety of salad on the side.

"Thy word is true from the beginning: and every one of thy righteous judgments endureth for ever."

Psalms 119:160

Moussaka

Fanette Morice

This savory Greek dish with layered eggplant smothered in a seasoned meat sauce and a thin béchamel is deliciously filling.

Serves 6

Ingredients:

5 eggplants (about 14-15 oz. each)

1 lb. 2 oz. ground beef

1 large onion (about 5 oz.)

1 cup olive oil (approximately)

2 1/4 cups whole peeled tomatoes (about 1 1/2 14 oz. cans)

1/4 tsp ground cinnamon

1/2 tsp ground nutmeg

1/2 tsp salt, 1/4 tsp pepper

2 Tbsp unsalted butter

2 Tbsp all purpose flour

1 2/3 cups milk

1 1/2 cups grated emmentaler cheese

1 Wash the eggplants, cut off the stems, and thinly slice them.

2 Layer the slices on a plate, salting each layer and covering with a paper towel before moving on to the next layer. Set aside.

3 Chop the onion. Heat 1 Tbsp oil in pan and lightly brown the onion for 3-4 minutes on medium heat. Add the ground beef and brown for another 5 minutes.

4 Stir in the tomatoes, and add the nutmeg, cinnamon, salt, and pepper. Cover and cook on low heat for 45 minutes.

5 Pour 1 Tbsp oil in a nonstick pan, add some eggplant slices, and drizzle 1 Tbsp oil over the top. Lightly brown each side on medium to high heat. Repeat the process for all of the eggplant slices. This will take awhile. Place the eggplant on a plate in several layers separated by paper towels.

Preheat a convection oven to 350°F.

Make a roux by melting the butter and mixing in the flour. Add the milk, stir, and bring to a boil.

Cook for about 5 minutes to thicken the white sauce.

6 Add a pinch of nutmeg and pepper. Add 1/2 cup of the grated cheese to the white sauce and melt.

7 Layer 1/3 of the eggplant in the bottom of a 9 x 13 inch glass dish. Spread 1/3 of the meat sauce on top, then 1/3 of the white sauce. Repeat the layers two more times.

8 Sprinkle the remaining 1 cup of grated cheese over the top. Bake for 30 minutes at 350°F.

Couscous

Farida Fons and Jacqueline Franco

This authentic and savory North African dish is a very hearty, festive meal.

Ingredients for 6:

3 small zucchini (1 lb. 4 oz.)
4-5 large carrots (about 1 lb. 5 oz.)
2 onions (8-9 oz.)
2 large garlic cloves
4-5 turnips (about 1 lb.)
1 whole clove
2 dried bay leaves
2 sprigs thyme leaves (or some dried)
1 full parsley sprig
kitchen string to tie the herbs
1 celery stalk
1 red bell pepper (6-7 oz.)
2 lbs. lamb chops or collar portions *(meat market)*
3 Tbsp sunflower oil
6 chicken thighs, skinned
3 chicken bouillon cubes
pinch of pepper, 2 tsp salt
2/3 cup double concentrated tomato paste
1 Tbsp couscous spice powder
2 1/2 cups canned chickpeas
3/4 cup raisins (optional)
harissa sauce in a tube (optional)
12 Moroccan or Mergeza lamb sausages-*meat market*
26 oz. couscous grain

1 Preparation: Peel the zucchini, carrots, onions, garlic, and turnips.

Cut the carrots in half lengthwise, then cut into long sticks.

2 Cut the turnips in half or in quarters. Stick one whole clove into one of the two onions.

3 Tie the dried bay leaves, the sprigs of thyme, and the parsley sprig together with kitchen string. If you don't have any sprigs of thyme, just sprinkle in some dried thyme leaves while cooking.

Wash the celery stalk and seed the bell pepper.

4 Cooking: In a *very large, deep pot*, brown the lamb chops in the hot oil. Set aside.

5 Brown the chicken thighs along with the onions.

6 Put the browned lamb chops back in the pot with the chicken.

Preparation

Cooking

Add the carrots and the turnips. Brown everything some more while stirring.

7. Heat 9 cups water. Take some of this water to dissolve the bouillon cubes. Pour the dissolved bouillon into the pot along with the rest of the hot water. Salt and pepper to taste.

8. Add the herb bouquet (bay leaves, thyme leaves, and parsley), the garlic cloves cut in half, and the celery stalk. Cover and cook for about 15 minutes.

9. Add the concentrated tomato paste and the couscous spice powder. Stir everything together.

10. Cut the zucchini in half lengthwise, then into long sticks and add them to the pot.

11. Add the red pepper cut into large pieces as well as the drained chickpeas.

12. Check the seasoning and add more if needed. Simmer on low heat for about 20 minutes.

If the bouillon is not strong enough, add more couscous powder to taste. Add the raisins at this time if you wish.

If you would like spicier sauce for your couscous, mix together some harissa paste from the tube with some olive oil and some bouillon from the pot.

When finished cooking the couscous, cook the mergeza sausages on the stovetop or in the broiler oven.

13. **For the Couscous Grain:** In a large pan, put 4 cups (26 oz.) couscous with 4 cups water. Add 2 Tbsp. olive oil and a pinch of salt. Mix together and put it in a hot oven (350°F) for about 10 minutes. The couscous will absorb all of the water. Take out the pan and stir with a fork to separate the clumps. Add 1-2 Tbsp butter.

Serve hot with the meat and vegetables and harissa sauce.

Cumin Meatballs

Cathy Scotto

These delicious, mildly spicy cumin meatballs remind us of far off places.

For about 20 meatballs

Ingredients:

1 1/2 slices stale bread, soaked in 1/2 cup milk
1 onion (4 oz.), chopped
17-18 oz. ground beef
5 oz. ground sausage
2 eggs
1 tsp salt
pinch of pepper
3-4 tsp ground cumin
1/2-1 cup flour
olive oil for the pan

1 Put the chopped onion in a large mixing bowl with the ground meats and soaked bread. Add the eggs, salt, pepper, and ground cumin. Mix together very well.

2 Form the meat into medium size balls. They should fit nicely in the palm of your hand. Roll the meatballs in the flour.

Brown them all over in a pan with olive oil until well cooked. Lay them on paper towels before serving.

Serve with couscous and a tomato salad with fresh basil.

For more authentic meatballs, replace the sausage with ground lamb meat. You can also add other spices like green anis seeds.

French Desserts

Cream Puffs

Annette Dure

This French pastry classic has a lot of steps, but the result is superb, excellent for any special occasion.

For about 28-30 puffs

Ingredients for the dough:
1 cup water
5 1/2 Tbsp unsalted butter
pinch of salt
1 Tbsp sugar
1 cup all purpose flour
4 eggs

Ingredients for the pastry cream:
2 cups milk
2 eggs
1/3 cup sugar
1/3 cup all purpose flour
1/2 tsp vanilla

Ingredients for the whipped cream (optional):
2 cups heavy whipping cream, cold from refrigerator
1/2 Tbsp vanilla
3 heaping Tbsp powdered sugar

The Dough:
Preheat oven to 350°F.

1 Pour the water in a saucepan. Cut the butter into pieces and add it to the water. Add the salt and sugar. Bring to a boil, then reduce heat.

2 Dump the flour all at once into the saucepan and stir into a thick dough with a wooden spoon. Place on low heat. Push firmly on the dough with one finger. It should not bounce back and should completely pull away from the sides of the saucepan and the wooden spoon. This only takes a few seconds.

3 Remove from heat. Add one of the eggs and work it into the dough well. Add each egg the same way. Be careful. If the eggs are slightly large, beat the last egg in a small bowl and add only one or two spoonfuls. The dough should be shiny and thick.

4 *You will know that the dough is worked well enough and that you have added enough or all of the last egg when you lift the* *spoon straight up from the dough and the peak that forms falls gently back down.*

5 Put the dough in a pastry bag and make small circles on a cookie sheet covered with parchment paper.

6 Take a fork, dip it in a small bowl of water and gently flatten the top of the circles in a crisscross pattern. Make sure to dip the fork into the water each time so it will not stick to the dough.

Bake in the middle of the oven at 350°F. for about 45 minutes. If the puffs are hard and do not give under slight finger pressure, stop baking. If they are not yet firm, you can lower the oven heat to 300°F and bake another 10 minutes to "dry" them out.

You don't have to do all the steps at once. You can make the puffs several days in advance. Store them in an airtight container. You can make the pastry cream and the whipped cream before serving.

The Pastry Cream:

Heat the milk in a saucepan on low heat to just under a boil.

7 During this time, put the eggs and the sugar in a mixing bowl. Mix with a wire whisk until foamy.

8 While mixing, sprinkle in the flour. Add the vanilla and stir again.

9 Add the hot milk to the mixture a little at a time stirring constantly.

10 Pour the whole mixture back into the saucepan that heated the milk. Bring to a boil on low heat while stirring constantly.

11 Let the cream thicken and let it cook while stirring for about 5 more minutes. Taste. If there is no more floury taste, the cream is ready.

Put it in a container with plastic wrap directly over the top to prevent a film from forming. Let cool and then put it in the refrigerator.

12 Cut the puffs in half. Put the cream in a pastry bag and generously garnish the bottom half of each puff with the cream.

The Whipped Cream:

13 Put all of the ingredients for the whipping cream in a deep mixing bowl.

14 Beat with an electric mixer until the cream becomes firm. This could take at least 5 minutes.

15 Pipe the whipped cream over the pastry cream of each puff.

16 Top each pastry puff with its other half.

Sift some powdered sugar over top of the finished puffs.

> *If serving with only pastry cream, there is no need to cut the puffs open. Simply fill them with the help of a pastry bag through a small hole made on the underside.*

> *For a finer textured pastry cream, use 1 whole egg and 2 egg yolks instead of 2 whole eggs.*

"Thy word is a lamp unto my feet, and a light unto my path."

Psalm 119:105

Chocolate Truffles

Fanette Morice

These deliciously rich chocolate bites will satisfy even the most demanding chocolate lover.

Makes about 40 truffles

Ingredients:

10 1/2 oz. (squares) semi-sweet baking chocolate (54% cocoa)
4 1/2 Tbsp unsalted butter
1 egg yolk
3 Tbsp sugar
2 heaping Tbsp crème fraîche (fresh cream)
1 tsp vanilla
cocoa powder, sprinkles, grated coconut, or other decorations of choice

Prepare all of the ingredients before starting. Cut the chocolate and the butter into large pieces. Separate the egg yolk from the egg white.

1 Dissolve the sugar with 4 Tbsp of water in a saucepan for 1 minute on low heat. Add the chocolate pieces and melt while constantly stirring.

2 Add the egg yolk *while stirring constantly* and cook for one minute on low heat. Remove from heat.

3 Immediately stir in the pieces of butter.

4 Stir in the fresh cream and the vanilla. Refrigerate for at least 4 hours or until solid enough to form balls.

5 Using two spoons or your hands, make small balls (about 1 inch). The chocolate mixture will tend to stick to your fingers until decorated.

6 Roll the truffles in cocoa powder, sprinkles, grated coconut, or any other decoration you choose.

*"Jesus saith unto him,
I am the way, the truth, and the life:
no man cometh unto the Father, but by me."*

John 14:6

Macarons

Base recipe

Annette Dure

Makes 50 shells (25 cookies):

Mastering these cute French cookies with a crusty top and chewy inside is the first step to an endless assortment of colors and flavored fillings.

Ingredients:

1 1/2 cups powdered sugar (*190 grams or 6.7 oz.*)

1 1/4 cups almond flour (*120 grams or 4.23 oz.*)

1/2 cup egg whites (*3-4 egg whites, 120 grams or 4.23 oz.*)

pinch of salt

1/4 cup white sugar (*50 grams or 1.76 oz.*)

Powdered or gel food coloring, but not liquid, any color

Because macarons require precise measurements, we strongly recommend that you weigh the ingredients.

Preheat the oven to 120° F. If your almond flour is not very fine, grind it together with the powdered sugar in a food processor using the pulse button.

1 Using a fine-screened sifter, sift the powdered sugar together with the almond flour onto a cookie sheet covered with parchment paper. *(This is the longest part, but very necessary to prevent lumps.)* Put this powdery mixture in the oven for about 15 minutes. Take out and let cool.

2 Add a pinch of salt to the egg whites. Beat the egg whites until stiff peaks form that don't fall back down. Sprinkle in the white sugar and beat for a few more seconds. *Note that if you want to color the shells, add some colored powder (about 1/8 tsp) or some gel paste (a small dab) after adding the sugar to the stiff egg whites and beat again.*

3 Add one third of the sifted almond flour and powdered sugar to the stiff egg whites. Mix the powders into the whites with a large flexible spatula in the following manner:

4 Always start at the center and turn under and up toward the outside left while turning the bowl to the right with the other hand. This process takes practice! Undermixing will result in a stiff batter. Overmixing will make it too runny.

Add the almond flour and powdered sugar two more times, mixing them in each time in the same manner. *When you spoon some batter out and drop it back into the mix, it should **very slowly** melt down and disappear into the rest of the mixture. It is often described as a "lava-like" texture.*

5 Fill a pastry bag with a 3/8 inch tip and make circles on an oven pan covered with parchment paper. The circles will spread out a little so be careful not to space them too closely together. Tap the bottom of the pan several times with a flat hand. Leave them sitting out for around 1 hour or until a small film has formed and it does not stick to your fingers when gently touched.

Preheat the oven to 320° F. Bake in the middle of the oven for 12 minutes. *Baking time depends a lot on your oven!* After 12 minutes, if the macarons are hard to the touch, take out of oven. If not, bake for 2-3 minutes more. You may need to try several times before knowing the best baking time and temperature for your oven. **Important!** *Let the macarons cool completely before taking them off the parchment paper.* They should come off easily without sticking. If the bottoms are not hard and smooth, they were probably not baked long enough.

You can keep them in an airtight container in the refrigerator for up to a week. Put the filling of your choice between two macaron shells before serving.

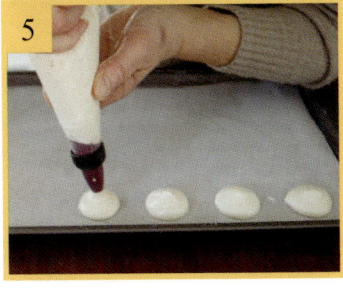

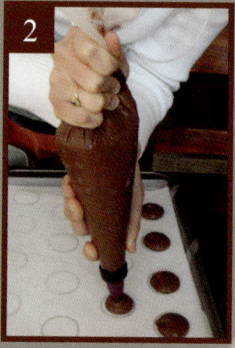

Tips for Beginners

Before you start draw circles in alternating rows on a piece of paper. The circles can be 1 1/2 inches or 2 inches in diameter. You'll need to leave about a 1 inch space between the circles. Make some tabs on one side of the paper with tape and slide this pattern underneath the parchment paper.

1 Prepare the pastry bag. Put a small piece of plastic wrap over the end of the pastry tip. Put the pastry bag in a large tall glass. This will let you work with both hands. Turn down the sides and fill the pastry bag.

Turn the sides back up and run your fingers from the top to push down any of the mixture. Remove the plastic wrap from the pastry tip.

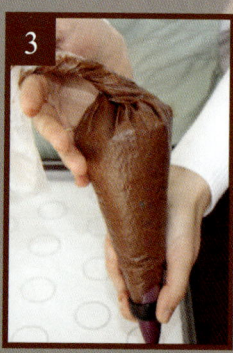

2 Holding the bag very straight, gently push out the macaron mixture letting it form a circle by itself without moving the bag. Stop filling the circle before reaching the drawn edges because it will spread out some when you stop. Lift off the pastry bag in a quick movement and go on to the next circle. *The tops should smooth out. If the tops have peaks, you undermixed the batter.* You can dab the tip of your finger in water and gently flatten the peaks.

3 As the level in the pastry bag decreases, twist the top of the bag.

4 Slide out the paper pattern by pulling on the tabs and use it as your guide on the next pan.

Chocolate Macarons

Annette Dure

This easy chocolate filling will definitely satisfy those chocolate cravings!

Ingredients for the filling:
3 1/2 oz. or squares semi-sweet baking chocolate (54% cocoa)
1/2 cup heavy whipping cream
1 1/2 Tbsp unsalted butter

Ingredients for the shells:
1 base macaron recipe
1/4 cup cocoa

1 Cut the chocolate squares into small pieces and put them in a small mixing bowl.

2 Heat the cream to just under a boil in a saucepan. Immediately turn off heat and add the hot cream about 1/3 at a time to the chocolate in the bowl. Mix in the chocolate pieces to melt them.

3 Add the butter and stir until smooth. Let cool in the refrigerator.

Make the base recipe for the macarons. **Note that you will need to sift the cocoa powder with the almond flour and the powdered sugar before** adding it to the beaten egg whites.

Let the chocolate filling soften slightly at room temperature before filling the macarons. Store them in an airtight container in the refrigerator.

Vanilla Buttercream Macarons

Annette Dure

This classic butter cream filling is simply delicious.

Ingredients for the filling:

2/3 cup milk

2 egg yolks

3 Tbsp sugar

2 Tbsp cornstarch

5 Tbsp and 8 Tbsp unsalted butter, softened

2 tsp vanilla

Ingredients for the shells:

one base macaron recipe

food coloring (optional) powdered or gel food coloring (not liquid)

Heat the milk very gently in a saucepan.

Whisk together the egg yolks and sugar. Continue mixing well for several minutes until pale and creamy. Add the cornstarch and mix again.

1 Add the hot milk slowly little by little into the eggs while stirring with the whisk.

Put the mixture back into the saucepan and let it thicken for several minutes on medium heat while stirring.

2 Remove from heat and add the 5 Tbsp of butter. Mix well until the butter is melted. Add the vanilla and mix again.

3 Put the cream into a bowl and cover it with a plastic film directly in contact with the cream. Let it cool at room temperature.

Beat the 8 Tbsp of softened butter in a small mixing bowl with an electric mixer.

4 Add the cooled pastry cream little by little to the butter while beating.

Make the base macaron recipe. Add the powdered or gel food coloring to the stiff egg whites after the white sugar if you would like colored shells.

Bake the macarons and let them cool completely before filling them with the pastry cream. Keep them in an airtight container in the refrigerator.

French Macarons

We kept the French name "macarons" to distinguish them from the American macaroons. France boasts many varieties of macarons that differ according to the region. However, this French macaron recipe, also known as the Parisian macaron, is a classic. Some say that macaron making is troublesome and very touchy, but we think that after a few tries and getting to know the best way your oven bakes them, you'll be just as addicted as we are! Be crazy about eating macarons, but don't let making them drive you crazy!

Lemon Macarons

For Lemon Macarons, add our Lemon Curd (see page 175). It's delicious!

Raspberry Macarons

Annette Dure

Although you can easily fill the shells with store bought jam, this easy homemade one is delicious!

Ingredients for the filling:
2 cups frozen (or fresh) raspberries
3/4 cup white sugar
1 Tbsp lemon juice

Ingredients for the shells:
one base macaron recipe
some red powdered or gel food coloring (not liquid coloring)

Mix together the raspberries, sugar, and lemon juice. Let it sit out for an hour. Place a small plate in the freezer for several minutes.

1. Put all of the raspberry mixture in a saucepan. Bring to a boil and let thicken for about 10 minutes on medium heat.

2. When you put a small drop of the hot mixture onto the slanted cold plate and it no longer runs after a couple seconds, remove from heat. Let cool at room temperature before filling the macarons.

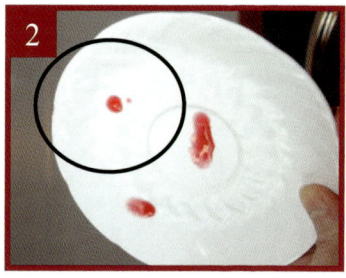

Make the base recipe for the macarons. **Note that you must add the powdered or gel food coloring after the white sugar in the stiffened egg whites as explained in the base recipe.**

Bake and let the macarons cool before filling. Keep them in an airtight container in the refrigerator.

Walnut Tart

Catherine Aramendy

This tart has little baking time, ideal during summertime, but also appreciated all year round. It is simply succulent!

Ingredients for 8:

1 puff pastry sheet, thawed
5 1/2 Tbsp unsalted butter
2 cups walnuts, coarsely chopped
1/2 cup sugar
1 packet vanilla sugar (or 1 tsp vanilla)
1 cup crème fraîche (fresh thick cream)

Preheat oven to 350°F. Carefully unfold and gently roll out your puff pastry on parchment paper. Cut an 11 inch circle of pastry. Place the parchment paper directly on a large cookie sheet or pizza pan. Bake for about 15 minutes.

1. Once the pastry is raised and golden brown, slide it off the parchment paper on to a pretty serving plate.

2. Put the butter, walnuts, sugar, and vanilla sugar or vanilla in a pan.

3. Cook on low heat while stirring constantly until the mixture caramelizes. Add the fresh cream and mix well.

4. Carefully spread this mixture on the cooled pastry. Wait 1 hour before serving.

Floating Islands

Fanette Morice

Small white islands floating in a sea of crème anglaise (vanilla custard sauce) is an easy, light dessert after a hearty meal.

Serves 6

Ingredients for the crème anglaise (vanilla custard):
3 eggs yolks
1/3 cup white sugar
2 cups milk
1 tsp vanilla

Ingredients for the islands:
3 egg whites
pinch of salt
1/4 cup powdered sugar

Topping:
Store bought or homemade caramel

1 **Vanilla Custard:** Vigorously mix together the eggs yolks and the white sugar with a wire whisk for a couple of minutes until pale and creamy.

2 Scald the milk by bringing it almost to a boil. Slowly pour it into the egg yolk and sugar mixture.

3 Mix gently, then pour it back into the saucepan on low heat.

4 If there is a layer of foam on the top, you can take it off with a skimming ladle. Cook on low heat for 5-10 minutes while stirring frequently until the cream coats the spoon.

5 When you can trace a line with your finger on the back of the spoon and it does not run or drip, remove from heat.

Stir in the vanilla and pour the custard into a dish to cool. Cover and refrigerate. Preheat the oven to 350° F.

6 **Islands:** Beat the egg whites with a pinch of salt until stiff. Add the powdered sugar and beat again for several more seconds.

7 Gently pack down the stiff egg whites into a buttered muffin pan or 6 small ramekins. Place the muffin pan or small ramekins into a larger dish. Fill the bottom of the larger dish with about 4 cups hot water. Bake the islands in this hot water bath for 10 minutes. The tops will lightly brown.

Vanilla Custard Sauce   *Islands*

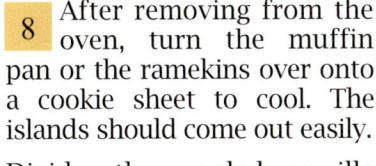

8 After removing from the oven, turn the muffin pan or the ramekins over onto a cookie sheet to cool. The islands should come out easily.

Divide the cooled vanilla custard sauce evenly among six serving bowls. Gently slide a knife under cooled islands to loosen them from the cookie sheet and float one in each bowl of custard. Drizzle a store bought or homemade caramel over each floating island. Serve cold. They can be made in advance and kept in the refrigerator.

Alsatian Christmas Spice Cake

Monique Ospel

This scrumptious secret family recipe from Alsace will certainly become a Christmas tradition in your family as it has in ours.

Ingredients for 24 squares:

1/2 cup raisins
1/3 cup candied lemon
2/3 cup water with 2 Tbsp imitation rum flavor
3/4 cup honey
1/3 cup sugar
7 Tbsp unsalted butter
1 packet vanilla sugar or 1 tsp vanilla
1 egg
1 tsp cinnamon
zest from 1 organic orange
2 cups cake flour
1 heaping Tbsp cocoa
1 1/2 tsp baking powder
1 1/2 Tbsp milk
2/3 cup chopped hazelnuts
1/2 cup sugar and 1/4 cup water (for the icing)

1 **The night before**, put the raisins and the candied lemon cut into small pieces into a jar. Pour the water with the rum flavor into the jar. Close, shake, then let them soak all night.

The next day, preheat oven to 350°F.

2 Melt the honey, sugar, and butter together in a saucepan on low heat. Pour this mixture into a mixing bowl.

3 Once the mixture has cooled off a little, add the egg, vanilla sugar or vanilla, and the cinnamon. Stir. Add 1 Tbsp of the liquid from the raisins and candied lemon, and the zest from the organic orange. Beat lightly with the whisk.

4 Sift the flour and the cocoa powder. Add them to the batter along with the baking powder and the milk. Mix well.

5 Add the hazelnuts, the drained raisins and candied lemon, while continuing to mix.

6 Pour the batter into a buttered and floured 11 by 7 inch pan. Bake for 25 to 30 minutes. Let cool in the

pan, then cut into squares.

7 Heat the sugar and the water in a saucepan on medium heat. Once the sugar melts and starts to boil, cook for about 5 minutes while stirring. Its texture will thicken like a syrup.

8 Turn off the heat and *rapidly* brush the icing on the cake squares with a kitchen brush. It hardens fast! When cooled, the icing turns white.

> *Prepare all of the ingredients in advance, including the sifted ingredients because this recipe needs to be mixed together rather quickly.*

Crêpes

Cathy Scotto

Here is the French crêpe in all of its simplicity. It is great for dessert, a snack, or family gatherings. But make several per person, because they will certainly be back for more!

Makes about 15-20 crêpes

Ingredients:

2 cups all purpose flour
3 eggs
pinch of salt
2 Tbsp oil
2 1/2 cups milk
1 Tbsp sugar
1 tsp vanilla
some oil for the pan

Preparation: Mix together the flour, eggs, salt, and oil with a wire whisk.

1 Add the milk little by little, mixing each time. Add the sugar and vanilla and mix together well with a wire whisk until smooth.

Cooking the Crêpes: Using a paper towel, rub a thin coat of oil on a 8 inch non stick pan. When the oil and the pan are very hot, pour 1 ladle of batter onto the pan with one hand.

2 Immediately and very quickly slant the pan with the other hand in a circular motion in order to evenly and very thinly spread the batter over the entire bottom of the pan. You might need to patch up a few holes until you master the technique.

Set the pan back on the burner and let cook on one side for about 1 minute.

3 Turn the crêpe over and cook the other side until lightly browned. Remove from pan and stack them on a large plate until ready to serve. Repeat the process until there is no batter left. Don't forget to rub a coat of oil on the pan each time.

You can fold them into fourths or roll them up for serving. Everyone can prepare their crêpes as desired. You can sprinkle the inside with sugar or powdered sugar, or you can spread them with jam or Nutella. They are also delicious with our lemon curd! (see p. 175)

🎩 It is better to make the batter ahead of time and leave it for 30 minutes or even a few hours in the refrigerator before cooking.

🎩 Sifting the flour will help prevent lumps. You could also mix it with an immersion blender.

🎩 The first crêpe usually flops when the pan is not hot enough or there is not enough oil.

"In the beginning was the Word, and the Word was with God, and the Word was God."

John 1:1

Far Breton
(Prune Custard Cake)

Raymonde Boëls

This simple dessert from Brittany is a family country-style custard.

Serves 8-10

Ingredients:

3 teabags, any kind
1 Tbsp imitation rum flavor
    (*optional*)
18 oz. pitted prunes
1 cup all purpose flour
1/2 tsp salt
3/4 cup and 2 Tbsp sugar
5 eggs
1/4 tsp vanilla
3 1/4 cups milk
1 1/2 and 2 Tbsp unsalted
    butter, softened
1 tsp cinnamon

1 Make tea using about 3 cups hot water. Add 1 1/2 tsp imitation rum flavor to the tea if you wish. Soak the prunes in this tea for 10-15 minutes. Drain.

Sift the flour, then mix together the sifted flour, salt, and 3/4 cup sugar.

2 Add the 5 eggs and the vanilla. Mix well with the wire whisk until smooth.

3 Heat the milk in a saucepan. When it is warm, add it little by little to the batter while continuing to stir. Add another 1 1/2 tsp imitation rum flavor if you wish.

Preheat oven to 410°F. Butter an 11 x 7 inch rectangular pan with 1 1/2 Tbsp butter.

4 Cover the bottom of the pan with the drained prunes. Squeeze them close together to fit them all in.

5 Pour the batter over top of the prunes to completely cover them.

6 Cut the 2 Tbsp butter into small pieces and place on top of the batter. Sprinkle with the cinnamon and 2 Tbsp sugar.

Lower oven heat to 300°F. and bake for about 1 1/2 hours.

7 The top will become golden brown.

The custard is done baking when a knife inserted in the middle comes out clean.

It is preferable to serve warm, but you can eat it cold as well.

"But as many as received him [Jesus], to them gave he power to become the sons of God, even to them that believe on his name."

John 1:12

Lemon Tart

Jacqueline Franco

Here is a classic French lemon tart that will please those lemon-dessert lovers.

Serves 8

Ingredients:

1 express pastry crust (see p.57) or 1 home made pie shell
3-4 organic lemons (*depending on how strong you want the lemon flavor to be*)
3 eggs
1/2 cup and 1 Tbsp sugar
3/4 cup heavy whipping cream
2 Tbsp almond flour
1/2 tsp vanilla
1 Tbsp cornstarch

Preheat oven to 350°F.

1 Flour the countertop work area. Roll out the pastry dough and sprinkle it with flour. Flour the 9 inch pie plate or 10 inch quiche dish as well.

2 Put the dough in the pan, prick it with the prongs of a fork, and cover the dough with a sheet of aluminum foil. Fill it with some dried beans, any kind, and blind bake it for about 10 minutes at 350° F.

3 Wash the lemons, then grate each one all over and place their zest in a bowl.

4 Sprinkle zest on the bottom of the pre-baked pie shell and set aside.

Squeeze the lemons and set aside their juice.

Put the whole eggs and sugar in a bowl and beat them with an electric mixer until foamy.

5 Add the whipping cream, almond flour, vanilla, cornstarch, and lemon juice one at a time, gently stirring each time.

6 Pour this mixture into the pre-baked pastry crust or pie shell.

Bake for 20-25 **minutes** at 350°F., then for another 5 minutes under the broiler *while watching attentively* until nicely browned.

Immediately take out the tart after 5 minutes.

Variations:

1) Make a meringue by beating 3 egg whites until stiff. Add 1/2 cup powdered sugar and continue to beat. Spread meringue over the lemon tart 5-10 minutes before the end of the baking time. Finish baking under the broiler while watching closely. Decorate with candied lemon pieces if you desire.

2) After baking for 20-25 minutes, sprinkle the lemon tart with sugar, then put it under the broiler for the remaining 5 minutes.

Chocolate Cake

Laura Canfran

Here is a deliciously rich, moist cake for chocolate lovers. And the best part is that you can make it all in the same pan!

Serves 8-10

Ingredients for the cake:

- 10 1/2 oz. or squares semi-sweet baking chocolate (54% cocoa)
- 11 Tbsp unsalted butter or margarine
- 1 1/4 cup sugar
- 3 1/2 cups cake flour
- 2 eggs
- 1/2 cup plain yogurt
- 1 tsp baking soda
- 1 cup hot water

Ingredients for the icing:

- 7 Tbsp unsalted butter or margarine
- 3 1/2 oz. or squares semi-sweet baking chocolate (54% cocoa)
- 4 Tbsp milk
- 3 Tbsp powdered sugar

You could add chopped walnuts or hazelnuts to the batter before baking.

The Cake:

Preheat oven to 300°F.

1 Cut the chocolate into pieces and melt directly in a sauce pan along with the butter on low heat. Stir often. Be sure not to let it boil!

2 Turn off the heat, add the sugar, then the flour, stirring each time.

3 Add the eggs, the yogurt, the baking soda, and the hot water. Mix together well. It's okay if the batter remains slightly lumpy.

4 Put parchment paper in a large rectangular 9 by 13 inch pan.

Pour the batter in and bake for about 45 minutes. The cake is completely baked when a knife inserted in the center comes out clean.

Set the cake aside while making the icing.

The Icing:

5. Using the same saucepan, melt the butter, then the chocolate broken into pieces. Add the milk and the powdered sugar. If the icing is a little too thin, add a little more powdered sugar to thicken it.

6. Pour the icing evenly over the top of the cooled cake.

Gluten-Free Chocolate Cake

Brigitte Kalms

This chocolate cake is deliciously gluten and lactose-free.

Serves 8

Ingredients for 8 servings:

- 5 eggs
- 3/4 cup sugar
- 5 1/4 oz. or squares semisweet baking chocolate (54% cocoa)
- 7 Tbsp unsalted butter, cut into pieces

Separate the egg yolks and the egg whites into two bowls. Add a pinch of salt (1/8 tsp) to the egg whites and refrigerate until needed.

1 Beat the yolks with the sugar until the batter runs from the beaters in a ribbon form. Set aside.

2 Beat the refrigerated egg whites until very stiff and put the bowl back into the refrigerator.

3 Break the chocolate into chunks and melt it in a double boiler or hot water bath on the stovetop. Watch carefully and stir constantly.

4 Once the chocolate is melted, remove from heat and add the butter cut into pieces. Stir together. (Keep out a piece of butter to grease the pan).

5 Take the bowl with the batter and add the melted chocolate little by little, stirring each time.

Preheat the oven to 390°F. (a convection oven if possible).

6 Pour half of the batter into the beaten egg whites.

7 Delicately fold in the batter with a large flat spatula, making a motion from the center of the bowl toward the outside edge. Gently fold in the other half of the batter.

8 Generously grease a 10 inch round cake pan or quiche dish with butter and pour in the finished batter. Tap gently on the bottom of the pan to evenly distribute the batter. Lower oven temperature to 350°F. Bake for about 25-30 minutes. Turn the pan around halfway through baking. Do not open your oven before then. Let cool before serving.

"Every word of God is pure:
he is a shield unto them
that put their trust in him."

Proverbs 30:5

Apricot Cake

Jacqueline Franco

From southern France, this delicious cake with melted caramel is a great recipe in which to use very ripe fruit.

Serves 8-12

We used a 10 inch diameter round cake pan

Ingredients for the caramel:

1/2 cup packed dark brown sugar
1/3 cup water

Fruit :

1 1/2 lbs. very ripe small apricots (18 for a 10 inch pan)

Ingredients for the batter:

7 Tbsp unsalted butter, melted
3/4 cup cake flour
1/2 cup sugar
1 Tbsp baking powder
3 eggs

Prepare the Caramel:

If you have a cake pan that can be used directly on the stovetop, pour the sugar and the water directly in the cake pan. (If not, use a sauce pan to make the caramel, then **immediately** pour it into the cake pan.)

1 Stir the sugar and the water constantly on medium heat until the sugar melts. When it starts to boil, cook about 7 minutes until the caramel has a thick texture and a deep caramel color. Be careful not to let it burn!

Spread it as evenly as possible on the bottom and the sides of the cake pan. Set aside to cool.

Cut the apricots in half and take out the pits.

2 Lay them out on top of the cooled caramel over the entire bottom of the cake pan.

Prepare the Batter :

Preheat oven to 350°F.

Melt the butter (without cooking). Remove from heat.

3 Mix the flour, sugar, and baking powder together in a bowl. Add the eggs and mix again.

4 Pour in the melted butter and mix once

more. Pour this batter over the apricots.

5 Bake for about 30 minutes.

Take out of the oven, cover the pan with a kitchen towel for several minutes, then gently loosen the edges of the cake with a knife.

Place an adequate sized serving plate upside down on the pan and gently turn both the plate and the pan over.

6 Remove the cake pan and place the cake on its serving plate in the refrigerator. Serve cold.

🧑‍🍳 You can make this cake all year round with a large 28 oz. can of small apricots when fresh ones are not in season.

Yogurt Cake

Ruth Morice

This classic French children's recipe is so easy because there is no need for measuring cups–just use the empty yogurt container as your measuring guide.

Serves 8-10

Ingredients:

1 container (4 oz. or 6 oz.) plain, vanilla, or fruit flavored yogurt
3 containers cake flour
2 containers sugar
1/2 container oil
1 packet vanilla sugar (or 1 tsp vanilla)
1 Tbsp baking powder
3 eggs

Preheat the oven to 350° F.

1 Put all the ingredients except the eggs in a bowl starting with the yogurt and then using the empty carton as your measuring cup.

2 Mix together well. Add the eggs and stir again.

3 Pour the batter into a buttered and floured 10 inch round cake pan.

Bake for about 45 minutes. Cover the cake with aluminum foil if the top starts browning too much.

See our Caramel Pineapple Upside Down Cake on page 162 which is actually an elaborated yogurt cake recipe.

Variation with Plain or Vanilla Yogurt

Take out 1/3 of the cake batter and put it in a small bowl. Mix in about 2 Tbsp of cocoa powder.

Spoon this chocolate batter in several spots on top of the other batter in the cake pan.

Lightly drag a knife several times in a zigzag pattern through both batters. You will thus obtain a pretty marbled pattern.

Other Variations When Using Plain Yogurt

Just before pouring the batter into the pan, try adding some of the following ingredients before baking.

-Cubes of fresh fruit such as apples or pears

-Chocolate chips and orange zest

-Diced pieces of fresh pears and chocolate chips (and orange zest)

-Pieces of dried fruit and nuts of your choice (raisins, apricots, walnuts, almonds...)

-Lemon zest and some squeezed lemon juice

-Apple pieces and cinnamon

French supermarkets offer a very limited selection of boxed dessert mixes. This versatile base cake with its many variations is practical in France because everyone always has yogurt in their refrigerator! They say you can even replace the yogurt with milk.
You might want to add a glaze or icing to finish it off.

Confiture de lait
Milk Jelly

Catherine Aramendy

Traditional milk confiture takes a couple hours to make. Here is the fast way that is so delicious you could eat it by the spoonful! Enjoy it on French bread, crêpes, ice cream, or pieces of fresh fruit. It's delicious with apples!

Ingredients:

4 cans of sweetened condensed milk (14 oz. each)

For each can you will need:

1 1/2 Tbsp regular butter, melted

1 packet vanilla sugar *or*
1 tsp vanilla

1 **Cooking:** Remove the labels and put the *unopened* cans in a pressure cooker. Add water up to the same level as the top of the cans. Close the pressure cooker and cook for 45 minutes after the pressure is reached. Let cool before opening the pressure cooker and taking out the cans.

2 **Preparation:** Empty the contents of one can into a bowl. Add the melted butter and the vanilla sugar or vanilla along with 3 Tbsp water. Mix together and put into decorated glass jars of your choice. It will keep for up to a month in the refrigerator.

Open the other cans and repeat the process or you can keep the other unopened cans in the cupboard. When you are ready to open a new can, it will be easier to mix the ingredients and the can's contents with an electric mixer because it will no longer be warm and soft.

You can also add 2 heaping Tbsp of ground hazelnuts to the finished preparation.

Eve's cake

Thérèse Jeanmart

This moist apple cake topped with slivered almonds is in memory of our dear sister in Christ, Theresa, whom we loved very much.

Serves 6-8

Ingredients for the batter:
5-6 apples, depending on size
1 Tbsp unsalted butter to grease the cake pan
1/2 cup cake flour
1/2 cup sugar
1/3 cup milk
3 Tbsp oil
1 1/2 tsp baking powder
pinch of salt

Ingredients for the icing:
1/4 cup unsalted butter, melted *or* crème fraîche
1/3 cup sugar
1 egg, beaten
1/3 cup slivered almonds

Preheat your oven to 350° F. Peel and cut the apples into cubes. Spread them on the bottom of a round cake pan.

1 With a wire whisk, mix together the flour, sugar, milk, oil, baking powder, and salt until the batter is smooth. Pour the batter over the apples and bake for about 15 minutes.

2 Mix together the ingredients for the icing while baking the cake.

3 Remove the cake from the oven and pour the icing evenly over the top. Sprinkle with slivered almonds and bake for another 15 minutes.

Desserts from Around the World

Sévillan cake
(Orange Cake)

Sylvia Garcia

This easy to make Spanish orange cake is very moist and delicious.

Serves 6

Ingredients:

8 Tbsp unsalted butter
3/4 cup sugar
1 cup all purpose flour
2 eggs
2 organic oranges
1 tsp baking powder
1/3 cup powdered sugar

Preheat oven to 350°F.

1 Mix the sugar and eggs together.

2 Melt the butter, then stir it in with the sugar and eggs. Add the flour and baking powder. Mix again.

Squeeze the juice from one of the oranges.

3 Separate the peel from the inner membrane and cut the peel into small pieces. Add the peel to the batter. Add the squeezed juice and stir.

4 Put the batter into a buttered 9 inch round cake pan. Bake for 30 minutes at 350°F.

Turn the cake out onto a serving plate. Stick the cake several times with a knife or a fork so that the orange juice in step 6 will absorb more easily.

5 Spread the powdered sugar on the cake.

Squeeze the juice of the second orange, and pour it over the powdered sugar.

6 Spread it over the top of the cake. Let cool before serving.

"And whatsoever ye do, do it heartily, as to the Lord...."

Colossians 3:23

Macrouds
Semolina Date Pastries

Viviane Delpuech

These sweetly rich, authentic Arab pastries smothered in honey are deliciously satisfying.

For about 30 diamond shapes

Ingredients for the date filling:

9-10 oz. pitted dates
2 1/2 Tbsp unsalted butter, softened
1 1/4 cup almond flour
1 tsp ground cinnamon
1/2 tsp ground nutmeg
1/2 tsp ground cardamom
1/2 tsp ground coriander

Ingredients for the semolina dough:

5 eggs
3/4 cups sugar
2/3 cups oil
2/3 cups milk
2 Tbsp orange flower water
6 1/3 cups fine grain semolina (2.2 lbs.)
2 tsp ground cinnamon
1 tsp ground cardamom
1 Tbsp baking powder
1 packet vanilla sugar *or* 1 tsp vanilla
3 cups honey

Date Filling: Slowly grind the pitted dates in a food processor. Add the softened butter and slowly pour in the almond flour while the food processor continues mixing.

1 Put in all of the spices and mix for a few more seconds. Set aside.

The Semolina Dough: In a large mixing bowl, beat the eggs with the sugar. Add the oil, milk, and orange flower water. Mix together.

2 Pour in the fine grain semolina, ground cinnamon, ground cardamom, baking powder, and vanilla sugar or vanilla. Mix again.

Preheat oven to 425°F.

3 Generously butter a 9 x 13 inch pan that does *not* have a nonstick coating. Evenly spread out half of the semolina dough.

4 Spread a layer of date filling over the dough. Cover this layer with the other half of the semolina dough. Bake for 20 minutes at 425° F.

5 Take the pan from the oven and cut parallel

lines across the pan.

6 Then, cut lines diagonally across the parallel lines. Finish baking for another 15 minutes at 390° F.

7 Take out the macrouds and glaze immediately with all of the honey. Let cool completely before serving. The macrouds will have absorbed all of the honey.

> *Dip your fingertips in some cold milk in order to smoothly spread out the top layer of semolina dough. The milk will also help the top turn golden brown during baking.*

> *Prepare all of the ingredients in advance so the dough does not dry out.*

Gazelle Horns

Agnès Delpuech

Serve your guests an authentic taste of Morocco with this sweet, almond-filled pastry and a strong, very sweet mint tea.

For around 40 pastries

Ingredients for the filling:

4 cups almond flour
1/2 tsp cinnamon
1 1/4 cup sugar
1 1/2 Tbsp unsalted butter, melted
7 Tbsp orange flower water

Ingredients for the dough:

1 3/4 cups all purpose flour
pinch of salt
1/2 cup orange flower water
2 Tbsp unsalted butter, melted

1 **Preparation for the Filling:** In a bowl, mix the almond flour, cinnamon, sugar, melted butter, and orange flower water.

2 Mix well. Keep working it until it becomes soft and flexible. Cover with a damp kitchen towel or plastic wrap. Set aside.

Preparation of the Dough: Mix together the flour, salt, orange flower water and the melted butter. Knead the dough by hand for about 15-20 minutes. *This is very important* so that the dough has a fine texture.

3 Take a small section of the dough and form a ball. Roll it out on a floured working surface, turning it over several times until it is *very thin.*

4 Form small rolls with tapered edges of about 1 Tbsp filling each and place on the dough. Fold over the rolled out dough in order to cover the rolls of filling.

5 Press hard with your finger to seal the edges.

6 Cut semi circles with a pastry cutter. Leave at least a 1/8 inch edge. *Rolling up the edges and pushing them down again will help prevent the filling from spilling out during baking.*

7. Gently curve each pastry into a half moon shape.

8. Prick each one several times with a toothpick and place them on a baking sheet brushed with oil or covered with parchment paper. Bake for 20 minutes one pan at a time at 340°F. They will not brown very much.

> Instead of hand kneading the dough for 20 minutes, mix the dough ingredients together, then use the kneading program on a bread machine.

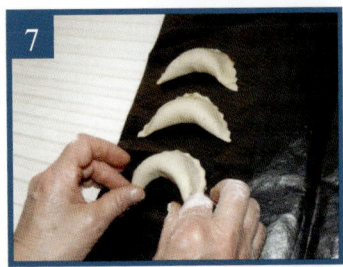

Nam Van
Tapioca Dessert

Esther Séphanh

This variation of a traditional dessert from Laos is a sweet mixture of unique textures.

Ingredients for 6 servings:

- 1 lb. fresh pumpkin
- 2/3 cup pearl tapioca, green or another color (Asian market)
- 1 cup and 2 Tbsp white sugar
- 1 can (13 1/2 oz.) coconut milk

1 Cut the rind off the pumpkin and cut the pumpkin into very small cubes.

2 Put them in a saucepan along with 2 1/2 cups water.

Bring to a rolling boil and add the pearl tapioca.

Lower the heat slightly and cook while boiling gently for about 10 minutes.

Stir frequently as the mixture will tend to stick to the bottom of the pan. Turn off heat.

3 Make the caramel following the pictures in step three.

4 Add the caramel to the tapioca mixture. Stir. *(Don't wait too long to add the caramel or it may harden.)*

5 Add the coconut milk as well and stir. The nam van will have a thick, soupy texture.

Serve warm or refrigerate to serve cold. It will have a more firm, pudding-like texture when cooled.

3 *The Caramel:*

a. Melt 2 level Tbsp of white sugar on low heat.

b. Let brown slightly.

c. Add 3/4 cup water, then 1 cup sugar.

d. Boil gently on low heat for 10 minutes to thicken the caramel.

4

5

> *Whenever making a caramel, stand back while adding the water to the caramel because it will splatter!*

> *You can make the dessert a day or two ahead. Refrigerate, then simply reheat if you wish to serve it warm.*

Caramel Pineapple Upside Down Cake

Jean Luc Thurard

This classic cake from the French West Indies is an elaborated yogurt cake. You'll love it!

Serves 6

Ingredients:

6 oz. pineapple yogurt—**use the empty yogurt container as your measuring cup for the following:**
3 containers of cake flour
2 containers sugar
1/2 container olive oil
3 eggs
1 Tbsp baking powder
2 tsp vanilla
1 tsp orange flower water
   (*optional, if you have it*)
1/2 tsp imitation rum flavor
   (*optional*)
1 tsp cinnamon
pinch of nutmeg
1-2 Tbsp caramel syrup
1 can (20 oz.) pineapple
   slices in syrup (about
   10 slices) *reserve the
   syrup*

Put the pineapple yogurt in a large mixing bowl. Using the empty yogurt container as your measuring cup, add the flour, sugar, and oil.

1 Add the three eggs, baking powder, vanilla, orange flower water, imitation rum flavor, cinnamon and nutmeg.

2 Blend everything together with an electric mixer for about 10 minutes. The mixture should be creamy.

3 Take two pineapple slices and cut into small pieces. Mix them into the batter. (*Keep 1/2 cup of the pineapple syrup for the end of the recipe!*)

Preheat oven at 350°F. Grease the sides only of a ten inch round cake pan.

4 Cut the other pineapple slices in half and place them on the bottom and the sides of the cake pan. Dribble the caramel syrup evenly over the pineapple slices. Pour all of the batter over the pineapple slices in the pan.

Bake in the middle of the oven for about 55 minutes, depending on your oven.

The cake is done when a knife inserted into the middle comes out clean. Take out the cake and put it on a cooling rack.

5. Run a knife all the way around the cake pan.

6. Using hot pads, set a large plate on top of the cake and turn over the cake pan and plate together. Leave it to cool with the pan still on.

Once the cake has cooled, gently remove the pan from the cake.

7. Pour the 1/2 cup of the pineapple syrup over the top of the cake. The cake will keep for up to 1 week in the refrigerator.

Tiramisu

Cathy Scotto

This easy, delicious Italian classic always pleases a crowd, but can easily be divided in half for a smaller party.

Serves 12

Ingredients:

1 1/2 cups strong coffee
2 cups cold heavy whipping cream
1/2 cup sugar
6 egg yolks
2 containers Mascarpone cheese, (8 oz. each)
2 packets vanilla sugar (or 2 tsp vanilla)
1 1/2 tsp orange flower water *or* 1/2 tsp imitation rum flavor
3 packages ladyfingers (about 24 per package)
cocoa powder to sprinkle
1 square baking chocolate

Pour the strong coffee in a shallow bowl. Let cool.

Beat the heavy whipping cream with an electric mixer until stiff. Place it in the refrigerator.

1 Combine the sugar and egg yolks in the top of a double boiler or in a hot water bath with gently boiling water. Cook for almost 10 minutes stirring constantly with a wire whisk. The yolks will thicken into a custard-like texture. Take off heat and stir in the mascarpone cheese, the vanilla, and the orange flower water or imitation rum flavor. Place it in the refrigerator to cool.

2 Line the bottom and sides of a 9 x 13 inch rectangular dish with plastic wrap. Dunk the ladyfingers *very rapidly* on each side in the bowl of cold coffee. Line them on the bottom of the dish and sprinkle the layer with cocoa powder.

3 Take out the egg yolk mixture from the refrigerator. Coarsely shave the chocolate squares with a knife over the bowl and stir.

4 Fold in the stiffened whipping cream.

5 Put half of this mixture on top of the first layer of ladyfingers.

6 Cover the entire layer of ladyfingers, then sprinkle again with cocoa powder.

7 Make another layer of ladyfingers dipped rapidly in the coffee. Cover this layer with the rest of the mascarpone mixture, then sprinkle with a final layer of cocoa powder.

Pull up a little on the edges of the plastic wrap to help retain shape and cover the dish with aluminum foil. Refrigerate for at least 6 hours.

Before serving, turn the dish upside down onto a serving platter. Remove the plastic wrap and decorate with sprinkles if you wish.

> Tiramisu is better when made the day before. You can even put it in the freezer for a few hours. Take out 1 hour before serving.

Note: Europeans use raw eggs in Tiramisu. This recipe has been adapted for food safety.

Carrot Cake

Kimberly Sauvage

This American recipe passed down through the years remains the most deliciously moist carrot cake.

Serves 12-15

Ingredients for the cake:

4 eggs
1 1/2 cups oil
2 tsp vanilla
2 cups sugar
2 cups all purpose flour
3 tsp cinnamon
2 tsp baking soda
2 tsp salt
3 cups grated raw carrots

Ingredients for the icing (optional):

8 oz. powdered sugar
4 Tbsp regular butter or margarine, softened
1 tsp vanilla
4 oz. cream cheese
1 1/2 oz. chopped nuts (optional)

Preheat oven to 320°F.

1. Mix together the eggs, oil, and vanilla in a large bowl. Add the sugar, flour, cinnamon, baking soda, and salt. Beat well with an electric mixer for about 4 minutes.

2. Add the grated carrots to the batter. Mix again.

3. Pour the batter into a 9 x 13 inch rectangular pan and bake for about 1 hour, depending on your oven. The cake is done baking when a knife inserted into the center comes out clean.

While the cake is cooling, prepare the icing. Put the powdered sugar, softened butter, vanilla, and cream cheese in a small mixing bowl.

4. Beat for about 2 minutes with an electric mixer. Add nuts if you wish.

5. Spread this icing on the cooled cake.

Variation

For about 12 large muffins

Instead of making one large cake, pour the batter into greased muffin pans.

Fill each one about 2/3 full.

Bake for 30-40 minutes, depending on your oven. Cool. Spread with icing and some nuts if you wish.

 *You may simply sprinkle the top of the cake with powdered sugar instead of icing.*

Christmas Cake

Viviane Delpuech

This elaborate English cake with homemade almond paste will delight both your eyes and your taste buds.

Serves 8-10

Ingredients for the cake:
2/3 cup candied orange peel
2/3 cup diced candied fruit
2/3 cup raisins
3 Tbsp freshly squeezed orange juice
1 1/2 tsp imitation rum flavor *(optional)*
11 Tbsp unsalted butter, melted
2/3 cup sugar
1 packet vanilla sugar or 1 tsp vanilla
4 eggs
2 1/4 cups cake flour
1 Tbsp baking powder

Ingredients for the almond paste (marzipan):
2/3 cup white sugar
3 3/4 cups almond flour
1 whole egg + 1 egg yolk
1/2 tsp vanilla
1 tsp lemon juice
2 cups powdered sugar

Ingredients for the icing:
2 tsp powdered egg whites
1 tsp lemon juice
2 cups powdered sugar

Preparation of the Cake:
Preheat the oven to 350°F.

1 Soak the diced candied fruit and the raisins in the orange juice and the imitation rum flavor.

2 Melt the butter and mix it with the sugar and vanilla sugar (or vanilla) in a mixing bowl.

3 Add the eggs one by one, mixing well after each egg.

While mixing, sift the flour over the bowl. Add the baking powder as well. Stir in the fruit and raisins along with their liquid.

4 Pour the batter into a greased 10 x 2 inch round cake pan. Spread the batter evenly and bake for about 35 minutes. After 10-15 minutes of baking, when the cake starts to brown, cover *with a sheet of aluminum foil for the rest of the baking time.* Set aside and let cool.

Cake Batter Preparation:

Preparation of the Almond Paste :

5 Melt the white sugar with 5 Tbsp water in a non stick saucepan. Bring to a rolling boil then remove from heat.

6 Stir in the almond flour. Let cool slightly.

Mix together the whole egg and the egg yolk along with the vanilla and lemon juice. Stir mixture into the almond flour and sugar.

7 Put back on the burner and cook for almost 5 minutes on medium heat stirring constantly. (The paste will easily separate from the sides of the pan.)

Remove from heat. Work the powdered sugar into the paste. It will be easier to knead it on the countertop.

Let it cool slightly on the countertop covered with plastic wrap.

8 Make a ball and roll it out the diameter of the cake.

Run a knife around the edges of the cake pan. Turn the cooled cake over onto a pretty serving dish.

9 Place the layer of almond paste on top of the cake and trim the edges evenly with a knife.

Royal Icing Preparation:

Mix the egg white powder with 2 Tbsp warm water. Set aside for about 5 minutes, then dissolve any lumps. Add the lemon juice.

10 Mix the powdered sugar *little by little in*to the egg white and the lemon juice until you obtain an icing texture, but not too thick or you will have trouble spreading it. You might not use the entire 2 cups of sugar.

11 Thinly spread the icing on the almond paste layer and on the sides of the cake. *Do this as quickly as possible because the icing hardens very rapidly.* Decorate the top as you wish. The cake keeps for up to one week.

Powdered egg whites are found in the baking aisle of your supermarket.

This recipe is adapted because the French traditionally use raw eggs in the almond paste and the royal icing. If you have an alternative recipe for the marzipan and the royal icing you can certainly use it.

Feuerwehr-Kuchen

Fireman's Cake

Diana Skender

This beautiful German cake does not take as long as it looks. It actually comes together with little effort.

Serves 8-10

Ingredients for the dough:
1 3/4 cups all purpose flour
1/2 tsp baking powder
1/2 cup sugar
9 Tbsp unsalted butter at room temperature
1 egg

Ingredients for the filling and toppings:
2 cans (15 oz. each) tart pitted cherries (2 cups in all)
1/3 cup cook and serve vanilla custard powder (*found by the pudding*)
1/2 cup all purpose flour
1/3 cup sugar
3/4 cup almond flour
5 1/2 Tbsp unsalted butter
2 pinches ground cinnamon (*optional*)
2 1/4 cups heavy whipping cream (refrigerate before whipping)
2 packets vanilla sugar (or 2 tsp vanilla)
some chocolate curls

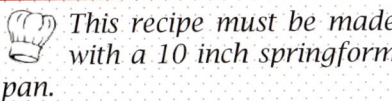 This recipe must be made with a 10 inch springform pan.

Cake Dough:

1 Mix the flour and the baking powder together.

Add the sugar, the butter cut into thin slices, and the egg on top.

2 Mix, then hand knead all the ingredients to form a ball.

Put parchment paper on the bottom of a springform pan, then butter the circle.

3. Spread out the ball of dough, pushing with your fingers from the center toward the outside edges. Push the dough up a little more than halfway on the sides of the pan.

4. *First Filling:* Preheat oven to 350°F. Using a strainer, separate the cherries from their juice. Put 1 cup of the juice in a saucepan.

5. Bring to a boil and slowly pour in the vanilla custard powder while stirring. Remove from heat while continuing to mix with a wire whisk.

6. Pour in 2 cups of the cherries. Stir.

7. Spread this thick filling on the dough.

> 👨‍🍳 *If the dough is too sticky, put it in the refrigerator for half an hour.*

> 👨‍🍳 *Be sure to push down well with your fingers on the seam between the dough on the bottom and sides of the pan. It needs to be the same thickness as the rest of the dough to make it easier to cut when you serve it.*

Crumbly Topping:

Put the flour, sugar, and almond flour in a mixing bowl. Cut the butter into slices and place it on top.

Knead the dough with your fingers. You can add a pinch of cinnamon if you wish.

8 Sprinkle this crumbly topping on the cherries. Bake at 350°F. for 40 minutes.

9 When done baking, run a knife around the edges before removing the side of the springform pan. *Let cool completely* before adding the next topping. *Put the heavy whipping cream in a deep bowl in the refrigerator ahead of time.*

Whipped Topping:

10 Remove the bowl of whipping cream from the refrigerator and add the vanilla or vanilla sugar. Beat the cream on high speed with an electric mixer (a food processor is even more efficient) until the cream becomes stiff.

11 Put the pan side back on the cake. Carefully and evenly spread the whipped cream on top of the cake.

12 Sprinkle with chocolate curls and a few pinches of ground cinnamon if you wish.

Remove the side of the springform pan and serve.

Zucchini Bars

Kimberly Sauvage

Here is one of the many variations of an American classic. Icing with a touch of cinnamon is a nice finishing touch.

Makes about 30 bars

Ingredients for the cake:
3/4 cup oil
1/2 cup white sugar
1/2 cup brown sugar
2 eggs
1 tsp vanilla
1 3/4 cups all purpose flour
1/2 tsp salt
1 1/2 tsp baking powder
2 cups peeled, grated zucchini
3/4 cup raisins (optional)

Ingredients for the icing:
3 Tbsp regular butter, softened
2 cups powdered sugar
2 Tbsp milk
1/4 tsp cinnamon

Preheat oven to 350°F.

Mix together the oil, white sugar, brown sugar, and eggs. Add the vanilla and mix again. Stir in the flour, salt, and baking powder.

1 Stir the peeled and grated zucchini into the batter. You can also add raisins at this time if you wish.

2 Pour the batter into a 10 x 5 inch jelly roll pan and bake for about 30-35 minutes.

Once the bars have cooled, mix together the softened butter, powdered sugar, milk, and cinnamon until smooth. Spread this icing quickly on the bars with a knife or a spatula.

Keep the bars in the refrigerator to prevent the icing from melting.

Lemon Curd

Jacqueline Franco

This delicious curd can be spread on bread, crêpes, and on the bottom of lemon tarts or other sweet pastries.

For about 5 small jars

Ingredients:

4 organic lemons
4 eggs
2 1/2 cups sugar
7 Tbsp unsalted butter, melted

Wash the lemons and grate the zest all over each lemon. Squeeze them for their juice.

Heat some water in a large pot for a hot water bath (bain-marie).

1 Beat the eggs in a bowl with the sugar. Add the lemon zest, then the melted butter. Stir vigorously with a wire whisk.

2 Add the lemon juice to the bowl while stirring to obtain a smooth mixture.

3 Pour mixture into a pan and place it in the hot water bath of gently boiling water. Stir constantly for about 30 minutes. The sugar will melt and the cream will thicken.

4 Pour the lemon curd into jars. Let cool before closing. These will keep in the refrigerator for 2-3 weeks. You may also seal them for a longer shelf life.

"The Bible contains the mind of God, the state of man, the way of salvation, the doom of sinners, and the happiness of believers. Its doctrines are holy, its precepts are binding, its histories are true, and its decisions are immutable.

Read it to be wise, believe it to be safe, and practice it to be holy. It contains light to direct you, food to support you, and comfort to cheer you. It is the traveler's map, the pilgrim's compass, the soldier's sword, and the Christian's charter.

Here Paradise is restored, Heaven opened, and the gates of hell disclosed. Christ is its grand subject, our good the design, and the glory of God its end. It should fill the memory, rule the heart, and guide the feet.

Read it slowly, frequently, and prayerfully. It is a mine of wealth, a paradise of glory, and a river of pleasure. It is given you in life, will be opened at the judgment, and be remembered forever. It involves the highest responsibility, will reward the greatest labor, and will condemn all who trifle with its sacred contents."

- Author Unknown

"Seek ye out of the book of the Lord, and read...."

Isaiah 34:16

Central Baptist Church

Perpignan, France

Formerly the capital of the Kingdom of Majorca during the 13th and 14th centuries, Perpignan, along with the rest of Northern Catalonia, was ceded to France by Spain in 1659. Perpignan has kept much of its Catalan culture and tradition including the language which is still spoken by a quarter of the population. Surrounded by the Mediterranean Sea to the east, the Pyrenees Mountains to the west, and Spain to the south, Perpignan's beautiful landscape is often dotted with vineyards. Many Spaniards and North Africans are a part of its growing metropolitan area with 300,201 inhabitants.

The Castillet (pictured here) in downtown Perpignan, originally constructed as a defense gate into the old city, later served as a state prison, and is now one of the major historical monuments of Perpignan. Our small church is only a five minute walk from the Castillet.

For about 30 years our church has rented a former car garage on the ground floor of a downtown apartment building. Our actual sanctuary is 700 square feet. Without any possible room to grow, we started considering the possibility of one day becoming owners of our own church building.

Please visit our website for more details about this cookbook project!

http://www.eglise-baptiste-perpignan.org

Click on the American flag for English

The members of the Perpignan Baptist Church have decided to give 10 % of the proceeds of this cookbook to the ministry of Tim and Elisabeth Knickerbocker in

Larodde, France

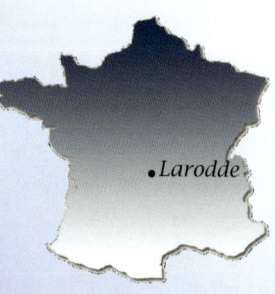

France is recognized as one of the most needy mission fields of the free world. Only about 0.6% of the French claim to know Christ as Savior. There is an urgent need for both national workers and missionaries from other countries. Part of their ministry is to help Americans enter the country, learn the language, receive essential training to adapt to the French culture, and become effective on the field. The following two pages briefly describe several programs they are developing.

Tim Knickerbocker came to France in 1971 as a student missionary. **Elisabeth** is French born. Tim pastored for 19 years in Toulouse, France. They started **Camp Rainbow** in 1987. While continuing their camp ministry, they began serving with Baptist World Mission in 2001, and are involved in itinerant evangelism and Bible conferences among independent Baptist churches in France. From 2004-2011 they helped found the Bible Baptist Church in Saint-Gaudens, now under national leadership. In 2009, they started the **Apollos Program**. After almost 40 years of ministry, they feel that the Lord would have them invest their time helping missionaries get to the field and become effective as well as training national workers for the Great Commission in France. The recent purchase of two large buildings in central France allows them and their associates to broaden these ministries.

For further information or donations contact:

Tim and Elisabeth Knickerbocker
e-mail: tim.knickerbocker@orange.fr
telephone: 011.33.473.21.59.42
camp website: http://camp-arcenciel.fr

Camp Rainbow

The Summer Immersion Program

Description: Throughout the summer, they hold several weeks of children, youth, and family camps at Camp Rainbow. If you are 18 or older, you may come and spend up to three months from mid-May through August. While helping at the camp in various ways, you could learn the language through daily contact with campers and personnel from all over France. Some tourism is included. This program gives a good taste of missionary life and French culture.

Requirements: Salvation testimony, baptized by immersion, and member of a New Testament church with the Pastor's recommendation.

Cost: $10 per day. This takes care of all expenses outside of personal purchases.

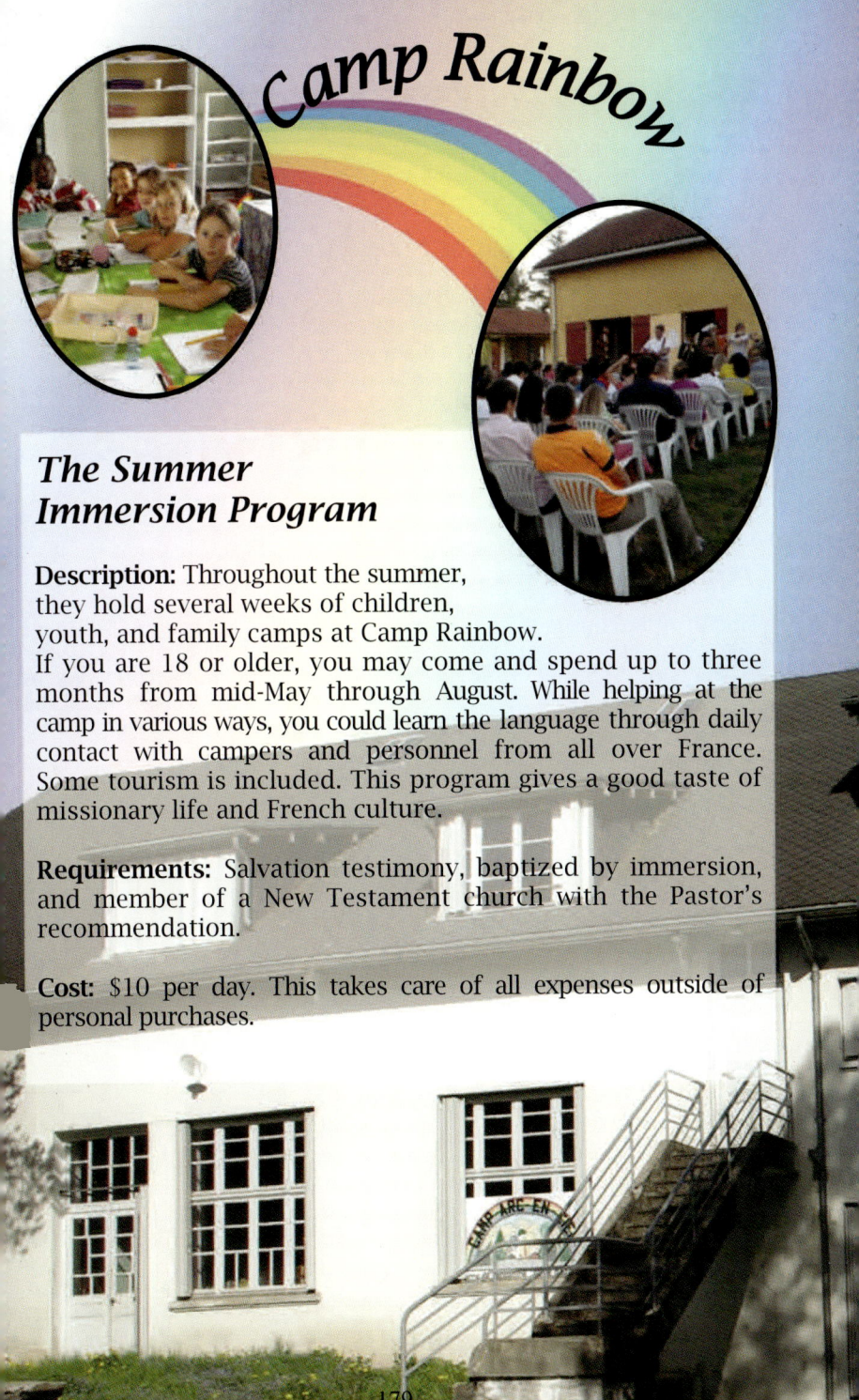

The Apollos Program

This one-year program (Sept—Aug.) is for training young people to become effective church leaders and helpers to pastors. It is a good immersion experience to discover if long-term missionary service is for you. It consists of:

1. 12 hours of Bible classes per week
2. French grammar instruction
3. Itinerant evangelism in churches around France as a team
4. Helping to manage Camp Rainbow and conference center

Requirements: Same as the summer immersion program plus a 1-year visa

Cost: $500 per month

The Fast Track Program

This program is specifically designed for college graduates who feel called to France or the French speaking world as missionaries. It is a two year program: the first year with Apollos and the second year in the Work Study program* as an apprentice to the Pastor in a local church setting. This program allows the participant to:

1. Learn the language before deputation
2. Meet the missionaries and personnel on the field
3. Determine if he can adapt to French culture for a long-term ministry
4. Engage in meaningful ministry and prepare an effective presentation for deputation
5. Develop a precise ministry project for future service
6. Benefit from counsel and evaluation from seasoned missionaries on the field

American churches interested in this program could reserve a small portion of their missions budget for a Fast Track candidate upon completion of this program and put him on a "fast track" for deputation.

Requirements: A ministry call, the intention to serve as a missionary, and the commissioning of the local church.

Cost: $1,000 per month

Larodde
Next exit: your future ministry

*The Work Study program is for training pastors and church planters. It consists of 3 years of 8 week cycles: 6 weeks in local church ministry and 2 weeks of intensive Bible class time.